TELL HER

She

CAN'T

ISBN 978-0-9859122-3-9 (paperback)
ISBN 978-0-9859122-4-6 (ebook)

www.gogirlpublishing.com
www.tellhershecant.com

Ordering information:
Special discounts are available on quantity purchases by corporations, associations and others. For details, contact info@gogirlpublishing.com

The events and conversations in this book have been set down to the best of the author's and interviewees' abilities, although some names and details have been withheld to protect the privacy of individuals.

DEDICATION

This one's for you, Koggy. We made it.

TELL HER *She* CAN'T

INSPIRING STORIES OF *Unstoppable* WOMEN

BY KELLY LEWIS

TABLE OF CONTENTS

CHAPTER 1

WHO SAYS *You* CAN'T?

*"Throw me to the wolves and I will return,
leading the pack."*

—Seneca (and Lisa Vanderpump)

C hances are that someone, somewhere, has tried to tell you that you can't.

Maybe you had a dream to be an astronaut, and everyone around you poo-pooed it, saying you didn't have the brain for that much math and science. Maybe you wanted to run a marathon, and your aunt told you that was a ridiculous idea for someone who could barely walk around the block. Maybe you thought of a business idea but your mom said it would never make any money. Whatever your ambitions or dreams, baby, the naysayers are everywhere.

I've encountered them my whole life, and I bet you have too. In the third grade, a boy in my class told me I could never beat him at the spelling bee. I stayed up all night studying and whooped his butt on competition day, despite fresh stitches from a dental operation in my mouth. In high school, a friend said I couldn't do more cartwheels than she could. I did 72 in a row and was still going, long after she had quit. I'm pretty much the poster child for "anything you can do, I can do better"—and I don't take kindly to being told I can't.

Throughout this book, we're going to talk about these naysayers—the ones I call the *blockmakers*. The people who stand in our way, get in our heads, and fill us with all kinds of self-doubt. If left unchecked, their limiting voices can become our own. We can't let that happen.

When you meet a blockmaker, you have two choices: accept their words as truth and give up, or use those words as fuel and prove them wrong. I hope after reading this, that you choose the latter.

Society has been telling women what they can and can't do, who they can and can't be, and what they can and can't look like, ever since Eve took a bite out of what I'm sure was a delicious apple. With that, women have been punished for eternity for their choices.

Can't focus too long on your career, you'll never have a family. *Can't* start a family, you'll ruin your career. *Can't* be too sure of yourself or you'll scare men away, *can't* be too accomplished or you'll be too intimidating—*can't, can't, can't*. Where does it end?

Trying to live your life by someone else's standards is a losing game, so I propose we change the rules. What if we started to hear "can't" as an invitation to do exactly that thing? What if we lived our lives exactly the way we want to, authentically and unapologetically?

We cannot control other people's opinions, nor can we continue to live life within boundaries that have been designed to keep us small. We are powerful. You are powerful.

You have the potential to take all the *hater-ade* around you and turn it into a propellant that pushes you toward success. You have the capacity to grow, learn, unlearn, and create so much beauty in the process. How do I know? Because I'm living proof.

I grew up in an environment in which I felt constantly on

edge, always on defense for the next attack. I've been drowned, smothered, and kicked in the stomach more times than I care to recall. I've experienced the effects of alcoholism, narcissism, and corruption. I've been devastatingly, heartbreakingly, betrayed.

The cards felt very much stacked against me for much of the first 17 years of my life, and no one would have judged me had I chosen to just accept this and live a muted life, never really reaching for the potential I knew I had within me. But I decided early on that I wasn't going to be a victim to my circumstances. I became determined to live a happy and successful life, and knew that one day, I would become even *more* successful than the people who had tried to tear me down.

No one else was going to determine my future—and no one can determine yours, either.

CHAPTER 2

WHO SAID $\mathcal{Q}$ CAN'T – AND HOW I DID

*"Although the world is full of suffering, it is also full
of the overcoming of it."*
—*Helen Keller*

I remember the first time my mother left me alone with them as if I'm looking at a series of Poloroids.

My small face pressed up against the living room window.

Tears forming in my wide brown eyes as I watch her pull out from the driveway.

My stomach falling as soon as she was out of sight.

We had just moved in with my mom's boyfriend (eventual husband) and his son to a house full of shadows in Austin, Texas. My parents had divorced when I was two years old, their marriage a casualty to alcoholism.

I kept mostly to myself in those days, hiding in my room except to steal one of my mother's chocolate chip cookies from the kitchen or to run free in our backyard, full of billowing trees and red ant hills.

The dark corners of the house tricked my mind, disorienting

me, leaving me always on edge, questioning everything. Was someone waiting for me outside of my room? Or was it the light?

With my mother gone, I knew I wasn't safe. I ran from the living room window to my bedroom, locking the door as fast as I could—but when I got inside I realized: I forgot to use the bathroom.

From my bed, I waited until I could hold it no longer before I dared creep back out, using one eye to scan the one-inch gap at the bottom of the door. Five minutes passed without a shadow moving. Then 10. Maybe I was being dramatic.

I turned the doorknob as quietly and slowly as I could, and tiptoed to the bathroom, careful to avoid any of the creaky spots on the floor. I had just about made it back to the safety of my room, when I heard the carpet crunch behind me.

Suddenly, my 11-year-old stepbrother had me by the ankles, suspending me in mid-air. I hit the floor with a thud and searched for any strand of carpet or wall to hold on to as he dragged me down the hallway.

The friction forced my shirt up around my chest, and, in my struggle to pull it back down, my hair became matted and tangled. My face flushed red in panic. I twisted and kicked to try to break free from his grip, as he pulled me to the foot of the couch.

Before I could even process what was happening, he picked up a blue pinstriped couch cushion, put it flat over my face, and pressed down as hard as he could.

The panic hit me first. My protests were muffled into the cushion; like trying to scream underwater. My asthmatic lungs spasmed for air, sucking fabric and cotton into my mouth. My nose was smashed to the side of my face.

Using all of the strength I could muster, I positioned my elbows onto the floor to give myself just enough leverage to sneak one breath of air. But as soon as I did, he straddled me, using his knees to pin down my arms at the armpit.

Terror and confusion ran parallel with my pumping blood. I didn't understand what I had done to him to make him so upset.

I didn't know how to make it better. I would ask myself these questions for many years to come.

"Hey!" my stepfather yelled from the other room. "What the hell are you doing?"

Tears of relief streamed down my face—help was on the way. I could hardly wait another second for him to pull my stepbrother off me, for this game to end, to be able to take a full breath again.

Instead, he laughed as he joined in, using his strong hands to hold me down by my ankles so his son could suffocate me even further.

Have you ever felt the shattering of your hopes so vividly that you could almost hear them? Like a glacier calving into the sea, I felt my spirit slide down, down, down into the floor right then. Beneath the beige carpet in need of vacuuming. Beneath the wooden floorboards and the dust mites. Beneath the foundation, the dirt and the worms.

And then, somehow, simultaneously, I was on the ceiling, watching my little body struggle to breathe under the weight of a grown man and his son. I was a pawn in some sick father-son bonding ritual, a tiny victim in a tug-of-war for power that I had no clue how to play, nor any chance of ever winning.

"Stop kicking," my stepfather said. "Stop kicking, and we'll let you up."

Smother—Revive—Smother—Revive.

I don't know how much time passed until they grew tired of this game, finally allowing me to scramble on my hands and knees back down the hallway and into my room. It could've been an hour. It was probably five minutes.

When my mother returned home that day, I shot out of my room wild-eyed and threw my arms around her waist.

"Don't ever leave me alone with them again," I cried, eyes swollen, on the verge of hyperventilating. "They put a pillow on my face. I couldn't breathe."

They snickered from the kitchen as my mother turned to face

them. I waited for her to fight for me, to scold them, to threaten to leave if they ever laid a hand on me again. I imagined us packing our bags and peeling from the driveway, the ice cream cones we'd share as we talked about those assholes and how glad we were that we got away. But the justice I hoped for would never come.

"Boys," she said. "Stop being nasty."

The messages that have ridden shotgun with me throughout the rest of my life began at that moment:

You are not safe.
You are not worthy.
No one is coming to save you.

As I got older, these messages were supported by a chorus of daily phrases, chanted to me by the two of them, behind my mother's back or when she wasn't within earshot.

You're fat. Have another serving, piggy. Oink oink.
You're ugly. What's wrong with you?
You'll never amount to anything.

This deep feeling of being unwanted and unsafe seeped into my bones over the years. It got just a little further inside me each afternoon when I'd come home to find my school photo the only one turned face-down on the family mantle.

A little further still every night, when I was woken up in the middle of sleep by a cup of water being thrown in my face.

Or a pencil.

Or a pillow.

Or a butter knife.

As I got older, these messages were supported by a chorus of phrases, chanted to me behind my mother's back or when she wasn't within earshot.

You're fat. Have another serving, piggy. Oink oink.
You're ugly. What's wrong with you?
You'll never amount to anything.

Those words hit the hardest. Yet with every cruel word spoken, a defiance within me ignited and grew a little brighter. My internal voice rose up as if to say: *you will survive this, and one day you will show them all.*

By the time I was in second grade, my mother and stepfather had expanded our family with two kids of their own, and we had moved to Hawaii; close enough to the beach where I could escape and find solitude.

I had a secret patch of sand that I pretended was all mine, at the end of the narrow, overgrown beach path down L'Orange Drive, just left of the plumeria tree. This small, circular area surrounded by *ākulikuli* succulents was my sanctuary, where I could write poems in the sand and imagine where the waves might take me if I let it all go and floated away on my back. It was there that I developed a close relationship with nature—and to my own power.

We lived on a small island street where the houses were always left unlocked. My neighborhood was home to adults who were known affectionately as my *aunties* and *uncles*. Us neighbor kids ran back and forth barefoot down the street until our mothers called us in after dark. On the weekends, we played hide-and-go-seek and performed plays for our parents, who grilled and drank beer together until midnight.

I hovered closely around the cookout table in those days, wondering why this version of my stepfather was one I never got to see at home. He could be so charming, so funny. Yet each night when the front door closed behind him, he changed back.

Some days, I would run across the street and play with my friend Rachel on her swing set as she'd tell me stories about Pygmies and Aborigines, stoking my curiosity about the rest of the world. Things never got better at home, but I got smarter, stronger, and more creative. I also got more defiant, angry, and more rebellious.

By high school, the toxicity grew so great that my stepfather and I could hardly stand to be in the same room. We fought constantly. I spent most of my time out of the house, working, or with my friends and my (much older) boyfriend, smoking cigarettes and whatever else we could find. One night, after a particularly scathing fight, I spilled out some of the poison that had been growing within me.

"I can't wait for the day you die," I said to him, slowly. Pointed. "I won't shed one single fucking tear for you." For the first time, he reeled backward, speechless.

That night there was a knock on my door. My mother took a seat at the foot of my bed. Her eyes were red and watery, and she struggled to make eye contact with me.

"I'm sorry things are the way they are," she said. "But you have two choices in front of you. You can let this destroy you, or you can use this as fuel to become better than they are."

My anger melted into the floor at that moment. For the first time, I could see her not just as my mother but as a woman—a woman in a second marriage that she was fighting to hold on to. A woman with an hourly-wage job who couldn't support three kids on her own. A woman who desperately wished things were better, but who didn't know how to make them so. My perspective on everything shifted right then.

If I wanted any kind of positive future for myself, I had to channel my hurt and anger into fuel, and use it as a force for good. It was in this environment that I realized that my determination could be my liberator. My obstinate nature was actually my protector.

Some people in life seem determined to try to tear you down, to hold you back, to steal your voice or breath. Don't let them extinguish the power and light that is you. Use it all as kindling to the fire of your resilience, and burn, baby, burn. One day, you will show them all.

What *Can't* Really Means

It's time we talk about "can't." This pesky, limiting word appears everywhere, whether other people are putting it on you, or if you're saying it to yourself. I'm certainly not the first person to talk about the word "can't," but since it's in the very title of this book, I feel it's important to explore more of what it really means. When you tell yourself, "I can't," chances are you mean one of a few things:

1. *I'm scared.*
2. *I don't know if I'm capable.*
3. *I don't want to.*

Let's look at these in turn.

1. You're scared

This is probably the most honest version of "I can't" and one that comes up for me frequently. I have noticed that when I say "I can't" to myself or to an idea, what I mean most of the time is that I'm scared.

I'm afraid of the potential of the idea and its outcome. I'm nervous about my ability to properly execute the work that it will take to create. For me, this initial gut-level response is a direct correlation to early trauma, when I began to form ideas about myself and my capabilities and was always scared of doing something wrong.

Over the years, I've learned to question this version of "I can't." When I say it to myself now, I try to catch myself and instead respond with, "Yes, you can," or, "You have everything you need."

2. You don't know if you're capable

It can be downright terrifying to try new things, especially if those things require you to put yourself out there publicly. Fear of failure always looms when we work toward things that seem unfamiliar and that we don't immediately feel all that capable of pulling off. We don't want to fail, so we just tell ourselves, "I can't."

Let's say, for example, you want to write a book. You feel this pull to start writing, but you don't have a title in mind yet, so you put it off and put it off, waiting for the title to come to you. You justify this time as "waiting for inspiration," when in the back of your head, you're just not sure you're even capable of being the kind of person who can write a book. The longer you wait to put words on the page, the louder your doubts become. Suddenly your inner blockmakers are firing off all sorts of unhelpful thoughts like:

> *"What makes you think you can write a book?"*
> *"It'll never be a best-seller, so why even try?"*
> *"Why even bother writing, you already have a good job!"*

I heard all these things from my inner critic in the process of writing this book, and I have had similar thoughts nearly every time I've tackled big projects in the past. So, I encourage you to respond to this restriction in a similar way: You are capable. You are strong. And you must start now.

3. You don't want to

Let's be real. Often, when we say we "can't," we mean we *won't*. We don't want it bad enough! We aren't willing to make sticky sacrifices or trade-offs. We aren't ready to be uncomfortable. We don't want to invest the time. We just plain *don't wanna*. And that's okay!

The push inside of you must be stronger than the pull outside of you. So stop telling yourself that you can't when you mean you *won't*. You could. You can. You are resourceful, powerful, and have every modern convenience available to figure it out. You just don't want to.

Too often, money is the reason we use to put off doing the things we're interested in doing. But if you really, *really* want something, you'll find a way.

I wanted to move to New Zealand so badly once that I sold everything I owned to make it happen—down to my rug and my toaster. I wanted to learn to snowboard but couldn't afford all the gear, so I asked everyone I knew if they had extra items that they had outgrown. They did!

Millions (literally, millions!) of women have pulled themselves out of debt, figured out how to become the first in their family to go to college, or used their resourcefulness to fund their dreams. You can, too.

Now that we've shaken the cobwebs off "can't" I want you to actively try, for the next week at least, to see how many times you encounter it. Catch yourself when you say it, and intentionally reword that sentence. Leave yourself little notes of encouragement around your house. Write them in the notes of your phone and read them before bed every night. *You can.*

The way that we speak to ourselves affects everything. When we tell ourselves that we can't, the universe echoes that back, and life becomes harder. Love is our default programming, but it can take us years to learn how to truly love ourselves. I learned this lesson, of course, the hard way—but once I finally understood it, everything changed.

When Loving Yourself is All That Matters

I've been climbing up a mountain in the Kingdom of Bhutan for the last four hours and the slog is endless. With each step through the dry red rocky dirt, my legs turn a little more to jelly. There's sweat pouring down my chest, and my lungs are screaming for air that I won't get hiking at this altitude.

At the top of this mountain, they say, is the Tiger's Nest, a majestic and sacred temple cut into the side of a cliff. The awe-inducing temple is one of the highlights to any trip to Bhutan, but getting there is no easy task: it's a five-hour hike uphill, no shortcuts.

At this point, I should probably tell you I'm also battling a wicked case of food poisoning.

"I think you need some water," Rinzin, my Bhutanese guide says, looking back at me with concern. "You're sweating."

Feeling queasy, I look up to see him, still wearing his traditional Bhutanese *gho*: a knee-length robe-like outfit with long sleeves, secured to his waist by a belt. He's carrying a backpack full of water *and* all my things, his forehead completely dry.

Crap, I think. *I might not be able to do this, after all.*

I feel the blood pulsing in the tip of my nose. The world starts to go a little foggy around the edges. How do I get myself into these situations?

"I can do this," I say out loud. "I can do this. I can do this. I can do this."

Back in New York, a few months earlier, I'd found myself looking at a map of the world. There, nestled in the Himalayan mountains, was a small country called Bhutan. The more I started researching it—how it's referred to as the happiest country in the world, and how the government makes decisions based on a philosophy called Gross National Happiness—the more I knew I needed to be there.

I desperately wanted to learn something more about myself, or the world, or how to heal my past hurts, before it was too late. So, I went—and soon found myself on a mountain, more confused and frustrated than ever, struggling to get to the summit.

"Have you ever had guests who couldn't make it to the top?" I ask Rinzin over dinner. He looks at me and smiles kindly. "Yes, but don't worry, Americans and Europeans almost always make it."

I *think* this bolsters my confidence in making it all the way up to the Tiger's Nest, but I'm not so sure. For those unable or unwilling to climb, there is another option: taking a horse. But the horse will only carry you halfway up the mountain, and *oh, the shame.* I hope I don't have to take the horse.

The morning of the hike, I wake up to what feels like a dragon clawing the inside of my belly. I reach for my phone to text two of my girlfriends.

"Up all night with food poisoning and diarrhea and am supposed to go on a five-hour hike, help, what do I do?"

I want them to say, "Stay in bed, it's not worth it, don't risk your health." But the part of me that's still a sucker for punishment knows that I'm going to get up and do the hike anyway.

"Yikes," they responded. "That could get messy. Take some

meds and toilet paper?"

And so…it's decided.

By 6 a.m., I am on the trail and hiking at a faster pace than I thought I was capable of. Time passes by rapidly, even though no one is talking.

"I can do this," I whisper to myself again, doubling over in crippling stomach cramps every 10 steps. "I can do this. I can do this."

I am half-in, and half-out of my body. Every now and then I forget where I am all together, until I look up, and focus on the temple. If you believe the legend, this is the site where Guru Rinpoche landed after flying in on the back of a tigress in the eighth century. He spent three years here in a cave meditating on how to subdue a demon and bring Buddhism to Bhutan, and the temple was built to honor this.

In 1998, the entire structure caught fire and burned to the ground. All that remained from the ashes was a small golden statue of the Buddha. Locals say they could see his face shimmering in the fire, defiant.

When Rinzin and I finally reach the temple, we are the first hikers of the day to arrive. A monk asks if I'd like to light the day's candle. The three of us sit quietly on the floor beneath the gold Buddha. Rinzin looks at me.

"I think that you have something in your heart that is bothering you," he says. This takes me by surprise. I keep my gaze fixated on the Buddha, feeling the scabs inside of me start to crack open.

"Life is like a dirty bottle of water," he continues. "The water in the bottle is pure and clean, but the outside of the bottle is dirty. Our job in this life is to do the work on ourselves until the bottle is as clean on the outside as it is on the inside."

I sit there for a few minutes, trying to absorb one of the most beautiful metaphors I have ever heard, something so simple it draws tears to my eyes. I let one drop from the eye that isn't facing Rinzin—a skill that I had perfected during my childhood—never veering my gaze from the gold Buddha.

TELL HER SHE CAN'T

So much has happened to me that I could not control. I spent so many nights of this life feeling unwanted and alone, begging for attention, begging for love. I never felt like I was enough. I close my eyes for one final moment, absorbing as much of the good energy as I can.

"We already love you," I hear a voice inside of me say. "Now you just have to love yourself."

I cry the whole way back down the mountain.

Why Other People Project Can't onto You (and What They Really Mean When They Do)

The thing is, when you grow up hearing that you can't, it starts to permeate. Feeling invalidated at an early age can sometimes mean you'll spend years searching for that validation in all the wrong places. It is imperative that right now, you begin evaluating the past stories you were told, and how and where they still live inside of you. Because as the saying goes, "hurt people, hurt people."

When other people tell you that "you can't," if they're well-meaning, chances are they mean one of a few things:

1. *Your idea scares me.*
2. *You are challenging the status quo.*
3. *I don't think you're capable.*

1. *Your idea scares me*

When you walk knowingly on the path of your own intuition and potential, it freaks the hell out of some people. So sometimes, their initial gut reaction is to say, "You can't." This stems directly from their own fear and usually isn't even about you.

Your willingness to act on your desires will rub some people the wrong way. There's really nothing you can do about this, except to realize that maybe these aren't your people after all. Or, maybe they are, and it's that the timing isn't right.

When people say "you can't," it sometimes means that they're scared of what might happen if you do. Who you are, who you choose to surround yourself with, and what you know to be true might change in your pursuit of this, and that might mean a shifting of power. It will almost certainly mean change, and change scares a lot of people.

2. You are challenging the status quo

Often "you can't" comes from a place of "I don't want you to" because you are challenging the status quo. You are making waves. You are changing. And that means that the people around you have to either support you or make way.

Our friends and families want the best for us, but many have been conditioned to believe that there is only one path forward: college, marriage, homeownership, kids. Anyone who tries to deviate from that path? Crazy.

Going against the grain, and therefore incurring disapproval, is an experience most of us will face. But as you'll learn through the stories in this book, initial resistance most often turns to support in the end.

3. I don't think you're capable

It's often the well-meaning who impose this version of "can't" upon us. In this capacity, what they are thinking is, "You might get your hopes up only to fail in pursuit of this, and I don't want you to go through that."

Remind them with love that you are capable and willing to try, and that there is no such thing as failure. So what if you "fail"? Failure is open to interpretation, and you are guaranteed to learn something in the process. To be human is to fail, and fail often.

There are also times we're told we *can't* by those who are not well-meaning, who are just trying to hurt us. Mean people really suck, and their words can sting.

The best way I've found to drown out their negative voices is to build a supportive network of people you can trust. Seek those who raise you up, and who fill you with laughter, love, and joy— even when they appear in the most random of places.

How Far and Wide the Journey

In 2017, I found myself riding on the back of a camel in the middle of a sandstorm in Jaisalmer, India, near the border of Pakistan. Coarse desert sand swirled around me, finding its way into my ears, filling my eyebrows, turning sweat into sand streams on my forehead. It must've been a hilarious sight, me struggling to pull my scarf closer around my face with one hand and hold onto a camel with the other. But Padam, my guide, just smiled.

As I surveyed the dusty dunes around me, I could only think of one thing: *I had come so very, very far*. Seven years earlier, I had launched my first business, Go! Girl Guides, a company that published the world's first series of travel guidebooks for women. Following that came the Women's Travel Fest in 2014, one of the world's first conferences for female travelers.

I was obsessed with traveling, so transfixed by the thrill of exploring new places that it enraptured me completely. The restorative feeling of a totally clean slate. The joy of viewing life through other perspectives.

So elated was I to spend hours wandering through markets, breathing in deeply the smells of cardamom and rose water, holding bags of spices to my nose.

Days without an agenda riveted me. Though I loved making new friends on the road, I took particular joy in traveling solo, knowing my own capabilities and instincts were enough to protect me. The world felt like a secret only I had access to, and I had everything I needed to absorb it.

When money ran low, I'd pick up odd jobs on the road or return home and bartend for a few months to make cash. Or I'd focus my efforts more on my travel blog and on freelance writing.

Each day of traveling healed my soul just a little bit more, restoring faith in me that the world *was* mostly kind, and that people *were* mostly good.

Chasing this wanderlust took me around the world to all seven continents and right back to myself. I felt the reclaim of a deep, primal fear as I jumped from the tallest bungee jump in the world in Macau; experienced the healing power of rain and movement as I laughed, dancing samba in the streets of Rio de Janeiro during Carnival.

I wondered in awe as I floated high above the Serengeti in a hot air balloon during the great migration; found myself discussing Greek mythology with an old friend at the foot of the Great Pyramids of Giza; climbed the Great Wall of China on complete accident, and realized just how small and interconnected we really are while camping beneath the stars in the Sahara Desert.

Here in India, a deep sense of gratitude permeated through every fiber of my body. If this was the adult life I got to live now, then the price I had paid in childhood was worth it. I was so free, so very far away, and so blessed.

"Kelly," Padam said, pouring us a cup of tea on the sand dunes after the storm. "Can I ask you a question?"

"Of course," I said. "Anything."

I readied myself for a question about my love life or why I wasn't married yet. Padam had shown me nothing but kindness when I found myself the sole guest in his hotel in Jaisalmer, a former fort city known as the "golden city," because of the way it appears to rise from the sand.

But he was still a man in India and no doubt had questions about why a young woman was here alone. Instead, he cracked a sly smile.

"What does a hot dog taste like?"

We erupt in laughter.

"I just always wanted to know," he said, shrugging.

Some questions will forever push you to seek answers. I may never know how to accurately describe the taste of a hot dog to a vegetarian (salty? chewy?), or why my childhood was so full of disappointment. I may never fully feel okay with words like "worthy" and "deserving," and I might always struggle with my weight.

I may never be able to forget some things. But I can try. I can heal, forgive, and reduce the power I give those memories. I can train my brain to stop when I start to think things like, "They were right, you'll never make it, you can't."

Because I know one thing for sure—tell me I can't, and I will.

CHAPTER 3

WHO SAID *they* CAN'T – AND HOW THEY DID

"Grief and resilience live together."
—Michelle Obama

It's one thing to tell you about the transformation I've lived through. But what about those who have experienced forms of adversity that I haven't? What about those who have overcome racism, cancer, domestic violence? Why is it that some of us are defined by our traumas while others use them as fuel to help them overcome?

Above all else, I am an optimist who deeply feels that anything is possible. I truly believe that you can have the life of your dreams no matter where you're from or what you've been through. But I wanted to test this on a wider scale.

In an attempt to better understand resilience, I started doing interviews. I reached out to a few women I knew who had been through trying times and made it to the other side stronger. These women didn't just survive, they thrived. Through their stories, I discovered the very powerful experience that comes from speaking your truth.

I began each interview with two questions:

Who in your life has told you that you can't?
Who did you have to become to prove them wrong?

Then, I listened.

During this process, I began to decipher specific strategies that helped these women overcome: mantras they told themselves to drown out negative voices, or survival tactics they clung to when it seemed nobody else was in their corner. Some of these methods were similar to ones I had adopted in my own childhood, and some were completely new to me.

Their stories blew me away, and the scope of this project grew. Those first women I had interviewed introduced me to others who inspired *them*, who sent me to a few more. And a few more. Before I knew it, I had interviewed over 100 women in the name of transforming trauma into power, and this project expanded to include a podcast and an online community, both called *Tell Her She Can't*.

My inbox was overflowing with messages from women who wanted to share their experiences to help lift others up—and it hasn't stopped. Weaving together these stories has revealed to me the very strength and resilience of the feminine spirit. This has become my life's greatest work.

Before you dive in, remember: we live in a society that encourages us to compare our traumas to see who "has it worse," and then negates everything else. Don't play into this victim mentality. Resist the urge to compare your struggles to anyone else's, and instead, keep your perspective on your potential. After all, it isn't the challenge that defines us—it's what we *do* with it.

This book was written to inspire you to take positive action in your life and to help you view life's inevitable rough bits as opportunities for growth. Every challenge, every pain, every life experience is valid—and all of it can be fuel.

If you feel triggered while reading this book, take a break. If you feel inspired, turn to our free downloadable workbook at tellhershecant.com/workbook to dig a little deeper.

The 35 women you'll meet in the pages of this book are of various ethnicities, and come from different backgrounds, cultures, religions, and corners of the world. Most have never met one another. Yet inevitably, someone, at some point, tried to tell each of them that they "can't"—and they each answered back, "Just watch me."

They are Changemakers, Champions, Warriors, Trailblazers, Adventurers, Visionaries, and Prevailers—and they share their stories of resilience here to inspire and remind you that you, too, are limitless.

THE WOMEN WHO *Refused* TO LISTEN

Challenging Systems to Create Impactful Change

THE CHANGEMAKERS WHO OVERCAME "YOU CAN'T CHANGE THAT"

"The people who are crazy enough to think that they can change the world, are the ones that do."

— *Steve Jobs*

I must've read the email a hundred times. It was 2014, and I was bartending in a basement dive bar in New York City's East Village, saving as much cash as I could to support my growing businesses. I was getting ready to open, alone except for the pizza cook in the kitchen and the mice that would occasionally dart out behind my feet. As I put the register together for my shift, my phone pinged. I read the preview in total disbelief:

On December 9th, 2014, the White House will host the 100 most influential travel bloggers and digital media outlets. We hope that you will join us at the White House.

It can be so hard to believe that you're on the right path in entrepreneurship, when that path also involves pouring shots of Fireball down the throats of 21-year-olds until 4 o'clock in the morning. This was exactly the validation that I needed. I was beside myself with glee and gratitude, dreaming about what it might be like as I tucked a bar rag in my back pocket.

Would I get to meet the Obamas? Did I need a dress?

I felt as though things were changing in my life—like getting the first glimpse of the finish line in a marathon. Two weeks later, I tucked my bar shoes into the back of my closet and boarded a bus to Washington, D.C.

At the White House, I sat in on discussions about the future of study abroad programs under the Obama administration. I listened as women I admired professionally took to the stage to talk about how travel had changed their lives, how it made them see other perspectives and realize they were but one small piece of the fabric of humanity.

To effectively create change, you must first be personally connected to the cause. As I walked past life-size portraits of some very powerful First Ladies in the East Wing, I started thinking about my own power, and what a huge role travel had played in developing and accessing it. Each day in a completely foreign place that I survived without incident was one more day that showed me my own strength. That I *could*.

The 100 of us at the White House that day were united by a common passion, and collectively, we helped put the spotlight on the value of study abroad programs. The hashtag from the event, #studyabroadbecause, generated over 63 million views on social media that day from our combined efforts.

I didn't get to meet the Obamas, but I did get a front-row seat to witness the arduous process of how change *actually* happens. Those who create lasting change are the ones who are courageous enough to speak out, and tenacious enough to keep pushing forward past the blockmakers who will inevitably say, "You can't change that."

The women in this chapter all know this first-hand. From lobbying Congress for greater access for the hearing loss community to raising millions of dollars for research on type 1 diabetes, these women are using their perspectives and lived experiences to make the world a better and more accessible place. These are the Changemakers.

REINVENTING FAST FOOD
SHANNON ALLEN

"When people tell me no it's almost like a green light goes off and I think, 'Oh, I should do this.'"

Photo credit: @aprilbellephotos

Shannon Allen is a singer/songwriter, actress, entrepreneur, creative, wife, and mother of five. She's the founder of grown™, a new chain of organic certified fast-food restaurants that serve real food through drive-thru windows. But before all that, she was a devoted mom with a big problem: something strange was happening to her 17-month-old baby, Walker.

"I realized that my middle child, Walker, had taught himself to say, 'Juice, Mommy,' overnight and that he was excessively thirsty," Shannon said. "He had peed through his diaper, he was lethargic, and he had started vomiting."

Shannon's husband is Ray Allen, two-time NBA Champion, 10-time All-Star, and a member of the Basketball Hall of Fame. At the time, the family was in Los Angeles for the 2008 NBA Championships.

At first, she chalked up Walker's symptoms to the crappy hotel food, or the time change and stress from traveling. But her husband asked her to promise that she'd have Walker looked at if he didn't return to his normal self by the next day.

The next morning, she woke up soaked in Walker's urine. He had completely peed through his diaper again, and as she put him in the bathtub, Shannon realized his body was as limp as a wet noodle.

She raced to call the hotel concierge and spoke with a doctor who suggested she take Walker to the emergency room. Before hanging up, the doctor insisted that she needed to ask the hospital for a blood test.

"Those were the words that would change my life forever," Shannon said.

For 25 minutes at the hospital, doctors tried to convince her that Walker was fine. Shannon pushed for a blood test, even when the doctor looked at her and said, "Fine, but you're going to be leaving here in twenty minutes with a prescription for Motrin." *So be it*, she thought.

"Twenty minutes later, the doctor comes back into the room, white as a ghost, tears running down her face," Shannon said. "And I just looked at her and said, 'Oh my god, you have bad news for me.'"

The range for normal blood sugars is between 70 and 120. Walker's blood sugar was 639. He had type 1 diabetes and had entered into ketoacidosis. His blood sugar was poisoning him to death. If they didn't get insulin for him soon, they were going to lose him.

"Over the next 48 hours, I had to become Walker's pancreas," Shannon said. "I was mixing insulin, I was giving injections, I was checking blood sugars between seven and ten times a day."

No one in their family had ever had diabetes, so she also had to quickly learn more about the disease. It was the scariest moment she'd ever had as a parent, she said, and everything else seemed completely irrelevant. The NBA Finals no longer seemed that important. Her own needs weren't anywhere in the picture. Everything from that point forward became about keeping Walker alive. As the family settled into their new normal, Shannon couldn't shake the feeling that this all seemed *wrong*.

"One day I thought, maybe this isn't normal and doesn't have to be like this," Shannon said. "Why, after over one hundred years, is insulin still the only therapeutic for diabetes? We can figure out ways to stop hair from thinning, we can figure out something to inject in our faces so we don't get wrinkles, but after all this time, we are still relegated to bloodletting our kids seven to ten times a day. This just, to me, seemed barbaric."

So Shannon, a former actress, threw herself into raising money to fund a cure for type 1 diabetes. She used every connection and platform she had. She spoke in front of Congress. She organized galas. She raised millions of dollars. But all this still wasn't enough to help her on the day she was running to the grocery store and noticed Walker's blood sugar level was falling—fast.

"I realized I needed food *now*," Shannon said. "I was searching for food that I could give my baby that would bring up his blood sugar, but not poison him. I needed real food and I needed it fast, and that's when I realized it didn't exist."

After frantically searching Route 9 near Wellesley, Massachusetts, and coming up empty-handed, she sped to a local restaurant, leaving her car running in the parking lot. She jumped over the counter and was able to find healthy food for Walker, just in time.

When she got home that night, Shannon sat on her shower floor and cried. For Walker's diagnosis, for her new reality. For the obstacles her family faced and those yet to come. She felt powerless and frustrated. And then she had an idea.

"I remember getting out of the shower and looking in the mirror and saying, 'Nobody is coming to save you,'" Shannon said. "I called my husband and said, 'Nobody has the balls to reinvent fast food, so I'm going to do it.'"

Shannon had gotten pretty good at creating healthy "pre-game meals" for her family before her husband's basketball games. She knew first-hand how food became fuel. What she was envisioning was healthy food, cooked slow and delivered fast, for busy people like her. She started writing a business plan and searching for investors. At first, all she heard was, "No."

"Everyone thought I was batshit crazy," she said. "They'd say, 'Fast food can't be reinvented, don't you think someone smarter than you would've done it already if it could've been done? Don't you think McDonald's would've done it?'"

But Shannon was no stranger to hearing "no" after years of auditioning for TV, film and the music industry, and she wasn't about to give up.

"Hearing no is just what happens to people, specifically women, and certainly women of color," Shannon said. "When people tell me no it's almost like a green light goes off and I think, *Oh, I should do this.*"

Eventually, she found seven people, all women, who invested in the idea. A full eight years after the initial idea, grown™ opened doors to a line that stretched around the block. They made three million dollars in revenue in their first year.

"Only two percent of businesses in the US ever make one million in revenue. We made a million dollars in sales in three months," Shannon said. "But we have a long way to grow. I'm not going to be satisfied until grown is accessible and affordable for every family, regardless of mean income or zip code. Grown is the future of fast food."

What started off as a very personal problem became a much larger mission that has now spread to three locations and counting. Walker, now 13 years old, and her children will always be her *why*.

"When I think about who I really am, besides being relentless, the person I really am is a writer," she said. "grown really is a love song I wrote about what I wish the fast-food experience could be for me and my family."

BIO: Shannon Allen (née Shannon Walker Williams) is a mom of five, singer/songwriter, actor, entrepreneur, philanthropist, content creator, and devoted wife to two-time NBA Champion, 10-time NBA All-Star, and Hall of Famer, Ray Allen. She was a member of Motown Records group, Shades, and has appeared in both TV and film *(Girlfight, Blues Clues, Century City, Sex and the City, Sesame English)* and can be found on Instagram at both @grown and @swalkerwil. In addition to her work creating and building an organic certified fast-food restaurant brand, grown™ (real food, cooked slow for fast people), Shannon has appeared on many shows, panels, and podcasts as a speaker, expert, and thought leader on entrepreneurship, organic food, health/wellness, parenting, and diabetes awareness. The Allens are passionate advocates for research for a cure for type 1 diabetes in honor of their 13-year-old son, Walker. Shannon, Ray, and their family devote their time and efforts to raise the level of awareness of type 1 diabetes and its symptoms and are committed with purpose, passion, and dedication to prevailing in the fight against this potentially life-threatening disease.

MAKING THE WORLD MORE HEARING-ACCESSIBLE
JANICE LINTZ

"Nobody walks between the raindrops."

Janice Schacter Lintz is a born and raised New Yorker. In 1994, her two-year-old daughter was diagnosed with hearing loss. The doctor delivered the news to Janice like it was a life sentence.

"He said, 'Don't worry, there are special schools for her,'" Janice said. "I hadn't even wrapped my head around this diagnosis, and suddenly the bar was lowered for her for the rest of her life, at two-and-a-half years old."

She walked out of the appointment furious, not about the hearing loss, but at the doctor for assuming that her daughter would live less of a life because of it.

So much of what she and her family loved about living in New York—experiencing the rich culture of the city's plays, theater, museums, and travel opportunities—suddenly came with new challenges.

That just would not do, Janice thought, and right then and there she made it her mission to help her daughter have equal access to everything in life. If her daughter's hearing couldn't change, then access within the city and even the very city itself would have to.

One day her daughter came down the stairs, defiantly announcing that she felt she didn't have to attend religious school anymore because she couldn't hear.

"Not so fast," Janice said. "Kids of all religions, from all over the world, have been trying to get out of religious school. That hearing loss excuse is just not going to work."

So, she went to the school to speak to the head rabbi, who asked her simply, "What do you need?"

To her surprise, after a quick discussion, the rabbi was able to implement and roll out new changes for hearing access. So she thought to herself, *well, if it's simply a matter of them not having the knowledge of what to do and needing education, what other organizations could I request changes from?*

"I thought well, if I could fix that so easily, maybe I can fix theaters and museums in New York City that easily," Janice said.

The temple where her daughter went to school included many wealthy congregation members, some of whom were prominent figures in government. Initially, Janice approached places that were connected to the temple and started having discussions about hearing access.

"If you want to enact change fast, and you don't want to spend a lot of money and you don't have a lot of people, you have to do things in a thoughtful and systematic manner," she said. "So, leveraging connections became the way I did everything."

When her daughter was young, she approached companies that catered to children, like the Big Apple Circus, to implement hearing access reforms. They did.

"I realized these projects take a long time, so I had better plan in advance," she said. "I started anticipating when [my daughter] would start traveling in New York City subways herself or taking taxis by herself. I started shifting that way based not on where she was, but where she was going."

But changing a mammoth and decaying New York City subway system was a big undertaking, and one that many people did not believe was possible.

"Most people told me it was not going to work," Janice said. "They all thought I was insane. But there is a lovely point in any big project, where you prove people incorrect, and suddenly you're not insane anymore. I love when people underestimate me."

Slowly but surely, she started making progress. By leveraging local connections creatively and by attending public meetings, Janice began pushing the city to become more accessible. She navigated city and federal legislation to ensure hearing access was incorporated into renovations or new buildings. Still yet, many people gave her the brush off. At least at first.

"I'm willing to work really hard, but I'm unwilling to permit people to spin my wheels," Janice said. "But after you start having successes, people start helping you because they realize, 'Oh okay, you're not wasting my time.'"

Soon, Janice became an expert at how to "short-circuit" the system, moving through the legalese in the most efficient way possible. She leaned on her own background as a lawyer to understand the system, using tips and connections to get in front of government officials and politicians.

"This didn't start out as a selfless endeavor," Janice said. "I had to change things so my daughter could function and so my family could function."

Pushing for change wasn't always easy, and it certainly wasn't immediate. At times, she didn't know if she'd be successful at all, especially on days when she was going through difficult personal challenges with her health or in her divorce. But she kept her eye on the big picture: doing whatever it takes as a mother to make life easier for her child.

Nine long years later, the New York City Taxi and Limousine Commission approved the voluntary installation of induction loops for people with hearing loss in New York City taxis and deployed the hearing access symbol on their vehicles, according to *The Hearing Journal.* The change made hearing access in taxis possible, which has benefitted millions of residents and visitors with hearing loss.

The Metropolitan Transit Authority (MTA) followed suit, adopting the hearing access symbol and installing hearing loop systems inside of 482 subway booths around the city.

But Janice hasn't stopped there. She's created the first federal definition of the statutory term, "Effective Access" by co-writing the National Park Service's accessibility guidelines for hearing loss.

She's worked with Virgin Atlantic and Delta Air Lines to add captioning for their in-flight entertainment, creating a best practice model that was later adopted by the U.S. Department of Transportation. She was even able to help convince Build-a-Bear to add hearing aids to their toy collection.

"Anytime you do something so dramatically different you have to be uncomfortable with knowing you see something other people don't," she said. "I was comfortable with being different. I was a mother, doing anything and everything to make life easier for my child and family."

A frequent traveler, she's now traveling the world looking for opportunities in which to improve hearing access both globally and here in the United States.

"Nobody walks between the raindrops," Janice said. "It's all about figuring how to reframe what seems like no way out into an incredible opportunity."

BIO: Janice S. Lintz is an accomplished consultant/advocate across the hearing access, advocacy, and related political spectrum. She is the CEO of Hearing Access & Innovations, which is the only company dedicated to helping the world's businesses, cultural and entertainment institutions, government agencies, and mass transit organizations improve their accessibility for people with hearing loss. She is also a travel/consumer education writer. She has traveled to 194 countries, territories, and unrecognized nations.

HELPING SHAPE NATIONAL
POLICY ON AUTISM
TAYLOR LINLOFF

*"It turns out I wasn't broken,
I just run a little differently."*

Taylor Linloff grew up in a world that felt like it didn't quite *fit.* They were "oversensitive," and thought of as the "weird crybaby kid." They had a range of specialty interests, transfixed by things like *Anne of Green Gables* and Nascar, things that nobody else seemed to care much about. Middle school, already full of awkward moments, was so emotionally exhausting and isolating that at times they considered suicide.

In their small town in Nova Scotia, home to a total of 3k residents, everyone knew each other, but few people really knew them. They kept themselves buried in books to get through it all. Even as a child, they had an extremely accelerated rate of reading, writing, and visual pattern recognition.

"I was a kid who was a target for bullies," Taylor said. "I was told by teachers I would have to try harder to fit in. I was told by gym teachers to try harder outside of class. I had hormonal imbalances, and the fact that I identified as queer, I was told, was simply a form of dealing with confusion."

One day, Taylor's mother was watching an episode of *The Nature of Things* with host David Suzuki, on the topic of ADHD in women. Their mother thought she recognized some similar behavioral traits in Taylor, so they decided it was time to really seek answers.

At age 23, a psychiatrist who specializes in developmental and neurological disorders finally diagnosed them. It wasn't ADHD. It was autism.

Suddenly, things started making sense. One in 59 people are on the autism spectrum, but too often, autistic women are ignored and forgotten. With a diagnosis, it was like everything clicked together. Taylor finally realized they weren't "weird" or "oversensitive." They had a diagnosis of autism spectrum disorder, and it didn't need to hold them back any longer.

"I felt validated," Taylor said. "It turns out I wasn't broken. I just run a little differently."

Still, the fact that it took so long to find answers, and the fact that women are so often misdiagnosed or overlooked and have to live through years of bullying before finally receiving an autism diagnosis, really frustrated them.

They didn't want others to have to struggle like they had. Forty percent of neurodivergent people have a related anxiety disorder, according to the Anxiety and Depression Association of America. So Taylor started wondering, "What can I do to help enact change?"

They happened upon an ad for a television program called *You Can't Ask That*, broadcasting nationally across Canada. The producers were looking for adults with disabilities across Canada to answer blunt questions from viewers. Taylor felt pulled to apply and was chosen to be a part of the show.

"I was picking up cards on camera and reading very blunt questions that people would never ask you to your face," Taylor said. "One of the questions was, 'Aren't you just odd?' I just laughed and said, 'That too.'"

It was the first time they had stepped out in such a public way with their diagnosis, but they knew it was just the beginning. Soon, Taylor began writing for *Autistics Aloud*, a digital and print publication written by and for members of the autism community, drawing upon their own personal experiences.

New science suggests that autism occurs in the womb during brain formation. Part of the reason autism is commonly thought of as being more prevalent in boys is because many of the original studies in the *Diagnostic and Statistical Manual of Mental Disorders (DSM)* have involved white, cisgender boys, Taylor said, and therefore men and boys are usually diagnosed more than women and girls.

"We are socially conditioned differently to boys," Taylor said. "We are still so lacking in our representation as autistic women."

Taylor knew there was still more they could contribute. So they started investigating what was being done with regard to autism at a national level. They saw that their parliamentary representative was working on a new project called the National Autism Strategy, but when they scanned the list of people involved, all they could see were stakeholders and parents of autistic children.

"Where were all of the autistics?" Taylor asked. "I reached out and said, 'I know your government is currently working on this strategy, but people like me aren't being represented. We're not being asked to come to the table.'"

The representative responded with an invitation for them to join the team. These days, Taylor is helping to craft Canada's national strategy on autism.

"The fact that I went from being an extremely bullied kid to being a published writer and being asked by a member of the federal government to speak on national policies is unbelievable," Taylor said. "A couple of years ago if you had told suicidal Taylor that they would be doing this, they wouldn't have believed you."

Taylor is now heading to college and plans on continuing to

help raise awareness of autism in women.

"I don't want any autistic girl growing up feeling like I did because they deserve to know that their difference is what makes them amazing," Taylor said. "We're one in 59, but one-of-a-kind."

BIO: Taylor Linloff is the creator of the *Aspirational Autistic*, a personal activism project. Taylor is a 25-year-old #ActuallyAutistic woman-aligned nonbinary person from Nova Scotia, Canada. They are available for conferences, events, and other advocacy-related works.

ADVOCATING FOR ACCESSIBILITY IN VENUES
GAELYNN LEA

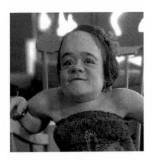

I'm here for a longer goal, and that goal isn't necessarily to further my career."

When Gaelynn Lea won National Public Radio's (NPR) Tiny Desk Contest (a nationwide contest that celebrates talented but undiscovered musicians) in 2016 and began touring the country, she realized America's music venues had a big problem.

Despite the Americans with Disabilities Act being signed into law in 1990, very few venues across the country were actually accessible for those with disabilities. As an artist with a disability who uses an electric wheelchair, that meant Gaelynn often had to be lifted out of her chair and on and off stage anytime she wanted to perform.

"I loved traveling and seeing the country and meeting all of these people, but it became really clear to me that the inaccessibility of most places wasn't just a problem in my hometown," Gaelynn said. "We were playing in big cities like New York and there was no bathroom that I could use, or I couldn't get in, or there were stairs just to get into the venue. Almost none of the stages were accessible, so they'd have to take me out of my chair and four people would lift my electric wheelchair on stage. After I performed, they'd have to help me down, which isn't really safe, is not dignified, and also isn't legal."

Born in Duluth, Minnesota, Gaelynn's fascination with music began when an orchestra visited her school in the fourth grade. She took a music listening test the following year and was the only student to get a perfect score. Her teacher looked at her and said, "Well, I have no idea how to modify an instrument for you, but let's give it a shot."

Gaelynn was born with osteogenesis imperfecta, also known as brittle bone disease, a condition that causes her bones to break easily. Many of her bones broke in utero, causing her limbs to be shorter than average.

First, she and her teacher tried to see if Gaelynn could hold a violin on her shoulder the traditional way, but even the smallest of violins were still too long for her. Then they tried the cello, but that was too large an instrument. Finally, they realized that she could hold the violin upright like a cello, positioning her hands as if she was playing upright bass. Gaelynn began playing in the school orchestra right away.

"People think that's the part of the story that's remarkable," she said. "But if you are disabled, especially the way that I am, you modify everything that you do all the time. The idea of modifying how I play the violin was not remarkable to me. What I realized a long time later, was that what *was* remarkable was that my teacher was willing to help me."

Unfortunately, not all her teachers were as supportive. When she reached high school, she had a music teacher who threw up his hands and basically said, "Well, I don't know what to tell you," and then left Gaelynn to figure out on her own how to advance in music. She continued to take private lessons, and by her senior year of high school, she was playing solos in the elite orchestra.

"Senior year that same teacher said, 'You know, when I saw you, I thought you'd sink or you'd swim and somehow you swam,' and this was after I had been one of the top students, and had just done a solo," Gaelynn said. "Saying, 'somehow you swam' felt very dismissive. It bothered me a lot, but it didn't destroy me, because I had a lot of supportive people in my life who were not sending me that message."

By 2016, she was working professionally as a fiddle instructor when her students told her about the NPR Tiny Desk Concert. Soon, her friends also started pushing her to apply. The third time someone told her about it, she decided to check it out. She applied, and she won.

"Never in my wildest dreams did I think I would win, because six thousand people from all over the country entered," Gaelynn said.

The prize was playing a Tiny Desk Concert in Washington, D.C. That performance has since been viewed over 3.6 million times.

As she played in D.C. and in four other cities, she and her husband started thinking about what it might be like to tour indefinitely across the country. Her husband had a full-time job, but the two knew there was more to explore in Gaelynn's music career, so they started planning for him to quit his job, after which they would sell their house, and tour full-time. But as they hit the road, they began encountering inaccessible venues almost instantly.

"I would go to a venue, and they wouldn't have a ramp," Gaelynn said. "So they would lift me up and I would play on the stage and then I would come back a year later, and they still wouldn't have a ramp, and they'd say, 'Oh well last year we just lifted you up.'"

Gaelynn realized this was becoming the new normal for these venues, and that in allowing them to lift her on stage, she was sending the message that it was okay for them not to update their infrastructure to become more accessible. So she drew a hard line in the sand right then and there: she would no longer let staff lift her out of her chair and onto the stage. If the venue didn't have a ramp leading up to the stage, she would play on the floor. If the venue wasn't accessible at all, she just wouldn't play there.

"I made this change not just for myself," she said. "I don't want them to be doing this in thirty years. So I figured if I started being really vocal about accessibility now, then hopefully for the next generation, things will be easier."

Many venues are still off-limits to her. Some have too many stairs at their entrance and no ramps, some don't have bathrooms that are accessible, and some have still not built platforms to their stages, despite ADA laws and guidelines. This has forced Gaelynn to be creative with where she performs.

"I've had to look at alternate venues like churches, which are often accessible," Gaelynn said. "I play all sorts of places, but the venues that *are* accessible but maybe didn't have ramps to the stage—a surprising number of them have built ramps. I am seeing some changes, which is very encouraging."

Her strong stance means she often has to say no to opportunities if they occur in venues that aren't accessible. Some of her friends and even other artists have questioned whether this might hurt her career, asking, "Isn't it better just to play and expose people to what you can do?"

"I'm here for a longer goal, and that goal isn't necessarily to further my career," Gaelynn said in reply to this. "There are other artists who are disabled who say, 'I feel like I gotta take what I can get,' and it does make me wonder, *Am I being too inflexible?* But the results of continuing to play in inaccessible venues does not lead to the change I'm looking for, so for the long-term, I'd rather make it harder for a while to hopefully make it easier later."

Making venues more accessible is one thing but changing the narrative when discussing disabilities is another. We in the United States still have a long way to go in that regard. So many disabled artists are making incredible art, but the narrative in the media often puts the focus on the disability instead of the art, Gaelynn said. Changing this narrative is part of the legacy she is building.

"I want to see disability viewed as diversity, and change the dialogue away from, 'Wow, they overcame this,' to what they're contributing to our society," Gaelynn said. "Disability culture is legit cool. We're making really good art, and it has a perspective that not everyone knows about. That's what I want the next generation to talk about. The disability narrative is often very one-sided and not celebratory, and I think we could make it more of a party."

BIO: Gaelynn Lea won NPR Music's *Tiny Desk Contest* in 2016, and not long after she hit the road with her husband, Paul. So far, she has toured in 45 states and nine countries, captivating audiences around the world with her unique mix of haunting original songs and traditional fiddle tunes. Gaelynn Lea has appeared in several major festivals over the years, including SXSW, Winnipeg Folk Festival, and Reykjavik Arts Festival. She has also opened for well-known bands such as Wilco, The Decemberists, LOW, The Jayhawks, and the industrial rock supergroup Pigface.

In addition to performing and recording, Gaelynn also speaks about Disability Rights, finding inner freedom, and accessibility in the arts. She uses her music as a platform to advocate for disabled people and to promote positive social change. In recent years, she has shared her perspective on PBS *NewsHour*, *The Moth Radio Hour*, *The Science of Happiness* podcast, and through two widely viewed TEDx Talks. Gaelynn Lea is currently working on a memoir about her touring adventures and disability advocacy that she plans to release in 2022.

SHE FOUGHT FOR HER RIGHT TO PLAY FOOTBALL, AND WON

RITA SCHMIDT

"There were a lot of times when I just had to rise above it. You just have to eat it and think, 'You know what? Twenty years from now I'll have a lot more to show.'"

When Rita Schmidt was in ninth grade, she wanted to play football on her high school's football team. But girls had never been allowed on the team before. In her bid just to be able to play a sport she loved, she faced coaches who claimed they didn't know how to accommodate female players, football players who didn't appreciate a girl coming onto the field, and high school mean girls who thought she was just playing to get closer to "their guys."

Change doesn't only happen on the federal level—it starts with each of us, and how we speak out within our own communities.

"My mom always made a point to fight for me to play in Pop Warner football, and she made a point to fight for me in high school when they had to take my request to the athletic director," Rita said. "Someone protested and said I wasn't allowed to play because I was a girl, and my mom stood up for me and said, 'Nowhere in the rule books does it say she can't play, so you have to let her.' A lot of those things happened behind closed doors, in the office with the athletic director and coach."

But winning the fight to play was only the beginning. After gaining approval from coaches who would have to make adjustments to ensure she had a women's locker room to change in, she faced her next barrier: the players.

"To this day I can remember in practice there were probably three guys that were actual gentlemen, not that they gave me any breaks, but they weren't looking to make it harder for me," Rita said. "But everyone else was like, 'Well we're gonna make this the hardest hit and maybe she won't come back.' Or they'd say, 'Well if she insists on playing then we're going to make her carry extra weight.'"

The parents of these players in her small hometown also had their own opinions. Some didn't love the fact that their boys were playing next to or across from a girl, or the fact that she was actually a good player, despite being one of the smallest on the field. Players on the opposing teams would often target her on the field when they played away games.

"I remember showing up to games and other players would spit at me, or grab my facemask and headbutt me," she said. "It would look like sportsmanship, but they would do it to be vicious. These were people I didn't even know, people from the other team, or when we'd get tackled, they would purposely throw a punch, or pinch, or elbow, or hold my facemask down to the ground for a little bit longer before I could get up."

But Rita was tough, and quick to suck it up and throw it right back to the players on the field. She learned how to hold her body differently, and how to position herself so that when she was tackled, she didn't break anything. She did just as many burpees and speed drills as everyone else on her team, proving that she was physically strong enough. By the time the season started, she was a starting player.

"I was on the starting lineup, I was a starting player, and that was also difficult for the people that were second and third string," Rita said. "It became, 'Coach is just doing it because she's a girl,' and in reality, it was that I was actually a good player. I had more experience under my belt than some of the guys."

Convinced that she had only started playing football to be closer to the boys on the team, some of the girls from her high school went out of their way to be cruel. As Rita was being crowned prom queen her senior year, one of those girls "accidentally" knocked her crown to the floor.

"This was straight out of a mean girls movie," Rita said. "I had to just smile and think, 'It's just a crown, it doesn't matter,' I remember having to stop to pick it up, and then putting it on later that night for photos with the prom king. There were a lot of times when I just had to rise above it. You just have to eat it and think, 'You know what? Twenty years from now I'll have a lot more to show.'"

Twenty years later, she does indeed have a lot to show—including a legacy that has helped pave the way for other girls to play football. Her time on the team shifted the policy going forward.

"For a long time, I thought maybe I was wired differently," Rita said. "But just last weekend, my old football coach stopped me and said, 'Oh by the way, my granddaughter is playing football now.' It's neat to see that twenty years later, other girls realize they can do that, too."

BIO: Rita Schmidt is a lover of all things outdoors and adventure. She lives in Benson, Arizona, where she works in accounting and enjoys hiking with her dog. The best way to get her to do something is to tell her it can't be done.

TOOLS TO TRIUMPH

These Changemakers were chosen for their intrepid insight and the ability to take active steps forward to improve their lives and, in the process, the lives of others. Here are some actionable ways that they got through the most difficult times.

To better implement these strategies in your life, remember you can always grab our downloadable workbook at tellhershecant.com/workbook.

1. **They rewrote the rules**

    When Shannon Allen was driving frantically up Route 9 trying to find healthy food for her diabetic son Walker, she suddenly realized it wasn't readily available. In that moment of desperation, she understood that fast food needed to be completely reworked and reimagined, but it had never been done. With no models to look to for comparison, Shannon had to use her creativity to rewrite the rules, inventing a new business and a new business model in the process. Too often we don't move forward when we can't see *exactly* where we're going. But moving forward on an idea is what *creates* the pathway. Rules are an illusion. How can you put a fresh spin on a problem you've encountered in your own life?

2. **They utilized the flaws of the system to their advantage**

On Janice Lintz's journey to help improve hearing access within New York City, she had to get creative in finding access points. She would study the local newspaper to see who was requesting money from the city, who was renovating, who was spending money, and where it was going. Armed with this knowledge, she approached project leaders to discuss incorporating accessibility into future projects or renovations. Some people thought she was crazy and that making New York City more accessible was impossible. She proved them all wrong by utilizing accessibility laws, taking it one project or business at a time, and never giving up. Can you employ this same tenacity in an obstacle you're currently facing?

3. **They wholeheartedly accepted themselves**

When Taylor Linloff was growing up in a small town prior to their autism diagnosis, they dealt with incessant bullying and isolation. Since their diagnosis, they have been on a journey to wholeheartedly love and accept themselves and all the wonderful things that make them unique. I love how they said, "We're one in 59, but one of a kind."

All of us have unique gifts to offer the world. What are yours?

4. **They stood firm in their beliefs**

Taking a stand for your beliefs can be challenging! Of course, there have been opportunities that have been difficult for Gaelynn Lea to pass up, but she knows that she's doing this work for the long term, and seeing change happen as a result of the position she has taken is gratifying.

From time to time we all find ourselves in situations that don't feel *right*. Others pressure us constantly to do what they want us to do. Do you have the courage to walk away, to follow the voice inside that questions, "Does this align with who I want to be?"

5. **They made decisions on what brought them joy**

In her pursuit of playing a sport that made her happy, Rita Schmidt had to contend with people who *weren't* as pleased about her playing it, including coaches, mean girls at school, and even other football players on the team. She could've chosen to give up doing something that she loved to do in order to please everyone else-but why should she have had to? Instead, she went after what brought her joy, regardless of the waves it made. She knew that any adversity she encountered wouldn't last forever. In pursuing a change in policy, women who have come after her have not had to fight the same battles. What brings you the most joy?

The CHAMPIONS

Finding a Purpose: Turning Adversity into Advocacy

THE CHAMPIONS WHO OVERCAME
"YOU CAN'T MAKE A DIFFERENCE"

"That which does not kill us makes us stronger."
— *Friedrich Nietzsche*

"If I ever catch you half-assing something again, I'll fire you faster than you can blink!" the owner of the small Portuguese bakery where I worked screamed at me, red-faced.

I was 14 and it was my first job, one that I secured part-time after finding out about a legal loophole that granted me a restricted work permit with parental permission. It was well after closing and I was doing my nightly cleaning rounds when he caught me stretching the vacuum cord a little further than I should have.

The outburst stunned me. My cheeks flushed and I stammered so many apologies while vacuuming the final patch of floor I had neglected, tears clouding my vision. As I rode my bike home that night, I was filled with rage. Who did this man think he was, speaking to me like this? Who did he think he was to treat any of his workers like this?

I watched my mother stress about money for most of her life. I knew that money equaled freedom. So, I kept my mouth shut while working at that bakery, saying nothing even when the owners made us do humiliating things like scrub the baseboards with toothbrushes. I was a good, hard worker—but 14 or not, I knew I did not deserve to be treated this way.

For a moment, I dreamed of what it might be like to have someone who could take up the fight on my behalf. An older brother I could run to who would defend me, or a dad to march in there and set him straight. Sadly, this wasn't my reality. If I wanted things to change, I had to learn how to use my own voice.

The next day I went to work, and before my shift started, I asked to speak to my boss privately. He closed the office door and we sat down. I could feel tears building hot with emotion behind my eyes, but I forced them down. I had something important to say.

"First of all, I understand what you were trying to teach me last night," I said. "But I am a good, reliable employee. I'm responsible. I've never even been late to a shift. And I want you to know that if you ever speak to me like that again, I will quit faster than you can blink."

I waited for him to react in anger or just fire me, but instead, I seemed to have earned his respect. He slowly nodded and apologized for how he had spoken the night before. I felt emboldened by being able to express myself, for once, without crying. This became one of my anchor memories—one I turn to when I need help managing my emotions during stressful moments.

That boss never spoke to me that way again. I set two rules for myself right then and there: I would never again sacrifice my emotional health for a job, and I would always speak out against injustice when I saw it.

Developing your voice goes hand-in-hand with finding your power. I've since spent a decade creating spaces in which women can share *their* voices and powerful experiences, whether on stage at Women's Travel Fest, as guests on the *Tell Her She Can't* podcast, or in the pages of this very book.

I consider the women in this chapter to be Champions—those who draw upon the personal circumstances of their lives to take up for others. Whether developing adaptive technology that provides independence to people living with disabilities or working to make a difference in adult oncology centers, these women have all channeled their life's experiences into energy that empowers communities, in spite of the blockmakers who have told them, "That's not the way it's done," or "You can't do that," or "That will never work." These are the Champions.

DEVELOPING NEW ADAPTIVE TECHNOLOGY
ADRIANA MALLOZZI

"People with disabilities are inherent problem-solvers because we have to be. The world is not built for us, so we have to figure out ways to work around those obstacles that we face day-to-day."

Adriana Mallozzi is an innovator, a tech entrepreneur, and an avid traveler. The founder of Puffin Innovations, she uses new technology and her own life's experiences to help positively impact the lives of others.

"I stopped breathing during the birthing process which caused brain damage resulting in cerebral palsy," Adriana said. "I am a quadriplegic, and I do everything with my head and/or mouth. And that's how I control everything in my life."

She grew up as a first-generation American born into an Italian immigrant family (along with sister Mickela Mallozzi, who is featured elsewhere in this book), and a strong work ethic was instilled in her from a very early age. She drew upon these lessons in childhood during hours of speech therapy, occupational therapy, physical therapy, and her school curriculum.

"We had such supportive parents," she said. "There wasn't a no in our vocabulary."

Adriana has always been determined to live her life as independently as possible. When she was seven years old, she was introduced to a piece of technology that allowed her to use a computer for the first time. That experience changed almost everything. Soon after, she got her first power wheelchair, allowing her much more independence and freedom.

"I really embraced technology at a young age, and I was just always thinking of how to improve things or how to make things better for myself and for others like myself," Adriana said. "People with disabilities are inherent problem-solvers, because we have to be. The world is not built for us, so we have to figure out ways to work around those obstacles that we face day-to-day."

In 2007, smartphones started making their way to the market. But Adriana couldn't use them yet, as they all had touchscreens.

"I would find hacks where I could jailbreak my phone and be able to control it using my computer," she said. "This idea of using my mouth to control technology was in my head also because I like to travel. When I travel, I typically bring my manual chair, and when I'm in my manual chair, I have no control of anything."

In 2015, she had the opportunity to take part in an assistive technology (AT) hackathon at the Massachusetts Institute for Technology (MIT), where she presented an idea in front of a panel of technology innovators and designers to create a wireless, mouth-operated device that could utilize technology to do everything from opening doors to setting alarms. It would be a game changer for the differently-abled community. The students at MIT agreed.

Ten hours later, the group had a prototype for the project—and with it, they won the hackathon. What followed was the creation and formation of Adriana's idea, and her company, Puffin Innovations, which produces assistive technology for people with disabilities.

"Unlike smart devices [on the market] right now, this is more about user predictability," she said. "We want to incorporate AI into the device, and over time as it is used, it will learn the patterns of the user, how they interact with the device specifically. People with disabilities, day-by-day, their bodies operate differently. First thing in the morning, they may be sitting up in their chairs, but then as the day goes on, they're slouching more. We want our device to notice that and then interact with that person."

Typical devices in the market are one-size-fits-all. But Adriana wants to change that model, instead creating specialized devices that put the user first. In addition to developing this technology, she's also working on an idea to create an inclusive, accessible coworking space for entrepreneurs with disabilities.

"As technology is evolving, it's easier and easier for people with disabilities to create their own businesses," Adriana said. "I just happen to be one of the lucky few who has had the opportunity to do that."

Though she has encountered many roadblocks to entrepreneurship, from investors saying no to developers who have tried to tell her things can't be done a certain way, Adriana won't be quitting anytime soon.

"There have been a lot of nos," she said. "But the nos just make me want to prove them all wrong. They're definitely fuel for me."

BIO: Entrepreneur, innovator, and disability advocate, Adriana Mallozzi combines her entrepreneurial spirit with a passion for technology and empowering people with disabilities. She started her first venture, My'deas, LLC, which soon became the parent company of myXpressions and My'Empowerment. Under My'Empowerment, she provides consulting services for caregivers and individuals with disabilities, helping them find the necessary resources to reach their full potential. In 2017, she formed Puffin Innovations, an assistive technology (AT) startup whose flagship product is an innovative, mouth-operated input device that incorporates machine learning, artificial intelligence, and IoT connectivity to give people with disabilities greater opportunities to lead more inclusive, independent lives. She is also working with a team to create an accessible, inclusive coworking space for current and aspiring entrepreneurs with disabilities, as well as small businesses/organizations that serve the disability community. It will be called Quirk LAABS (Leveraging Abilities to Achieve Better Solutions).

Adriana is a guest lecturer at Northeastern University and Boston University Physical Therapy and has led occupational therapy/AT classes for over 10 years. She has also appeared on numerous panels covering topics ranging from assistive technology, disability advocacy/inclusion, and entrepreneurship for venues including HUBweek, ATIA, MIT, Olin College, and SXSW. She also serves on the Board of Directors of Easterseals Massachusetts, and on the Advisory Board for HackerU.

SHE USES HER PASSION AND PURPOSE TO UPLIFT OTHERS
DR. FROSWA' BOOKER-DREW

"I don't want to be a person who, when leaving the planet, leaves all of these possibilities of things I could've done."

In 2005, Dr. Froswa' Booker-Drew lost her father and her uncle in a matter of days. At the cemetery, a friend turned to her and said, "This place is a gold mine of dreams that never were realized. Is that going to be you?"

It was right then and there that she vowed to live her life to the fullest. No matter what had happened in her past. No matter what was to come at her in the future.

She went back to school in her 40s with a young daughter at home and got her PhD in leadership and change, becoming the first in her family to earn this level of degree. She published three books and became a TEDx speaker.

"All of us are here for some purpose," Froswa' said. "My dad was this amazing cook. He could've been [a great chef like] Emeril, but because he didn't deal with his own demons, they dealt with him. I took all of that and I said, 'I don't want to be a person who, when leaving the planet, leaves all of these possibilities of things I could've done.'"

Life wasn't always easy for her. As a young African American girl growing up in the 1970s and '80s in segregated Shreveport, Louisiana, she was bullied incessantly by other girls in her class.

Her father, once a prolific chef and beloved member of the community, went bankrupt and turned to alcohol. Then the family home caught fire.

"My clothes smelled like smoke, I was just trying to fit in and my hair was falling out," she said. "When you're in ninth grade and you have this serious stuff that's going on at your house, at the time you don't see this as, 'Oh, this is fuel.' At the time you just want to get out of it."

But it *was* fuel, pushing her forward. To get through it all, she leaned on her mother and her community at church. She got more comfortable with public speaking by delivering speeches and making announcements to the congregation on Sundays.

"That was the beginning of me finding my voice," Froswa' said. "I got a lot of love from folks who looked like me, but who were not really wealthy. These were salt-of-the-earth folks who pushed me and told me that I could do whatever I wanted to do, even though I was hearing other voices at school that said I couldn't."

Froswa' understood early on that education was going to be her way out of Shreveport, and her path forward in life. In high school, a teacher at school encouraged her to run for school office. She did, and she won. It was her first glimpse into leadership and change, and what role she could play in creating that change.

Froswa's passion for community service has remained ever since. It followed her to college at the University of Texas at Arlington, where she became president of her dorm, and ultimately the president of the NAACP on campus, winning a national award for her leadership. It continued as she worked with the non-governmental organization (NGO) World Vision.

And it continues today. Froswa' is currently the vice president of community affairs and strategic alliances for the State Fair of Texas, the largest fair in the United States. The fair brings in over $50 million annually, but the site upon which it is held is surrounded by impoverished communities. Her work helps to make sure that some of that money gets invested back into the neighborhoods that surround the fair, through educational programming and community development. She and her team have championed initiatives that have provided grants and funding to over 60 organizations.

Through this work, she has positively affected the lives of thousands of people—which is especially important right now, as the COVID-19 crisis severely and disproportionately impacts minority communities.

"A lot of our smaller Black and brown nonprofits are not getting the support they need," Froswa' said. "In Dallas, there aren't many Black women who are in positions of power to give money. So, I aim to do what I can do to help lift other people up."

It's these sorts of challenging moments that so often shape us. Though losing her father and uncle so close together was devastating, it pushed Froswa' to seek meaning and opportunity at every moment in life and create a lasting legacy in the process.

"I realize now the impact on my daughter of watching me pursue my PhD," Froswa' said. "She is such a strong, beautiful, vocal young woman and because I shared with her what I was learning, I believe it empowered her to follow her dreams of becoming a photojournalist. I realized my power and the importance of following your dreams because my dad did not reach his. It was because of his life and his death that I vowed not to let my passion and dreams waste away."

BIO: Dr. Froswa' Booker-Drew is the author of three books for women. In addition, she is the host of the podcast *The Tapestry*, designed for women to share their stories of tenacity, tragedy, and triumph. Froswa' is an adjunct professor at Tulane University, the vice president of community affairs at the State Fair of Texas, and the cofounder of HERitage Giving Circle. For more information about Froswa', visit drfroswa.com. Or follow her on LinkedIn.

HELPING CHILDREN WITH LIMB LOSS
LESLIE PITT

"What could've been my greatest loss has become my greatest gift."

Leslie Pitt was six years old when, on the first day of summer vacation, she was hit by a dump truck carrying gravel through her neighborhood. The impact crushed her left leg and it had to be amputated.

"I woke up in intensive care, and my mom and dad came to my bedside and told me what happened," Leslie said. "I remember my mom telling me that my leg had been amputated. She said, 'It means your leg is gone and it will never grow back,' and in my mind I was like, 'Okay, that is what it is.'"

Though she had to spend the summer in rehabilitation, Leslie and her family were determined for her to continue living her normal life. She set her sights on the next year of school, and all of the new adventures that would come with returning.

"I was determined that I was not going to miss the first day of second grade," she said. "I went back to the same classroom with my new little prosthetic leg and cane, and to all my friends I was no different because I was still Leslie. I just now had a prosthetic leg."

Though her prosthetic leg made it more difficult to play certain sports, the rest of her childhood carried on relatively undisturbed, due, in part, to her family who refused to allow her to use her leg as an excuse. She had a lot of support around her, but there were still some who seemed to believe she couldn't do certain things.

"There was always that underlying mentality that some people held because I walked with a different gait," Leslie said. "It was like, oh she can't do it, and I was always like, well actually I can. Tell me I can't, and I will prove you wrong."

Leslie has carried that same mentality into adulthood. After a trip to Africa with her brother, she decided to explore what more she could do for children within the limb-loss community. In certain parts of the world, being an amputee means being socially condemned, ostracized, or even thought of as a witch and killed.

"My value as a human is no different because I grew up in the United States and not in Guatemala or Ghana," Leslie said. "Looking back, I was very fortunate, and I feel like I've been pretty fortunate into adulthood, so I try to pay that forward."

She founded a global nonprofit called Project LOLO (Love Ourselves, Love Others) that partners with clinics in developing countries to help children get access to orthopedic care and devices such as wheelchairs and prosthetic limbs.

Her involvement in the limb-loss community has also helped push her forward through difficult times. After the Boston Marathon bombing, Leslie spent time with a family with a little girl who had lost her leg.

"I remember so clearly that the mom and dad had this look of anguish on their faces," Leslie said. "And then the dad said, 'You have given us so much hope because we see what she will be like in thirty years.' And of all the things I've done, I would relive the last thirty-five years to have somebody say that again. It really made me want to get more involved with kids and kids with limb loss."

Recently, Leslie authored a children's book, *Lolo's Superpower*, about a toy named Lolo who looks different from all the other toys in the toy store. Lolo loves being different and celebrates it as their "superpower." Lolo makes all of the other toys want to celebrate their differences as superpowers, too.

"When I think about it, what is the common experience that we all have as humans?" she questioned. "It's loss. Part of the human condition is that at some stage of our lives we experience some kind of loss. Whether it's the loss of a leg, like me, or the loss of a loved one, or a job, whatever that is, it's part of being human. What could've been my greatest loss has become my greatest gift."

BIO: Leslie Pitt has been called a "globe-trotting humanitarian," but she started out as a little girl who dreamed of making the world a better place. She is educated in law, nursing, biology, global health, and human rights. After a 25-year healthcare career, Leslie shifted paths to pursue her passion helping children with differing abilities by creating the global nonprofit organization Project Lolo.

When Leslie was six, she lost her left leg above the knee. She knows what it is like to be a child longing to be seen for who she really is, beyond her differing physical abilities, or "disability." She wrote the children's book, *Lolo's Superpower* to help children embrace differences that make them unique.

ONE WOMAN'S WORK
TO INCREASE REPRESENTATION
IN BRANDING
WILLOW HILL

*"It wasn't people telling me I can't,
necessarily, it was that no one
throughout my life had told me that
I could."*

As a Native American woman raised by a single mother, much of Willow Hill's formative ideas of herself were influenced by the questioning that seemed to constantly arise with regard to her name and heritage.

"As a child, I was surrounded by people that were prejudiced toward indigenous cultures. They'd ask me, 'What are you?'" Willow said. "My relationship with my identity started and evolved through this. I started asking, 'Who am I and where do I belong?'"

Her mother had her at age 16 and worked non-stop while putting herself through college to provide for Willow and her sister the best that she could.

"I grew up experiencing a lot of racism which was hard to process," she said. "I knew the reaction that my name and my race evoked, and I knew from such an early age that in order to be accepted I had to change what that was. I started lying about my race, I said I was from Hawaii."

She loved to write, but often it seemed that the more she tried to produce in school, the less her teachers believed she was capable. Once, in middle school, she stayed up all night working on an essay. She wrote it and rewrote it, enlisting her mother's help with editing, and feeling so proud of the end result. A few days later, the teacher called both Willow and her mother into the office.

"She sat me down and said, 'This is plagiarized,'" Willow said. "I was devastated. It's moments like that, where people are saying 'I don't expect this of you, so it can't be true.' Those are the small moments where you are held back in really big ways."

Still, Willow knew she was meant for more. She picked up multiple jobs as a teenager and continued to work her way through college. As she entered the journalism program at the University of Oregon on a scholarship, Willow found herself thinking more and more about the impact that brands have in terms of representation, and the way they encourage us to view ourselves and each other. Then she thought back to her own upbringing.

"It wasn't people telling me I can't, necessarily, it was that no one throughout my life had told me that I could," Willow said. "Representation really matters. If people who are building solutions and putting companies into the world don't resemble the population, then you have a really big gap. The lack of representation for women, and specifically women of color, is everywhere: the executive level, political system, books, advertising, movies, and TV. It's pervasive."

She has made it her mission to change that in her career, working with brands to integrate purpose and diversity into their operations. She was an early employee at Airbnb and worked to help build a global and inclusive brand rooted in belonging. She also began to get more in touch with her own personal power, embracing the qualities that made her unique. She deepened her connection to her Indigenous roots, and she never forgot how it felt to be constantly singled out and questioned for her name or heritage.

Today, she's the cofounder of a creative agency called Scout Lab, which focuses on building and scaling purpose-driven brands. She is vocal about inclusion, diversity, and representation. Part of the work she does includes putting companies that are women or minority-owned in front of her network of venture capitalists and angel investors.

"The narratives we are exposed to impact our ability to relate, and have compassion and empathy," she said. "My business was built on the premise that the right stories need to win. In order for that to happen, the right stories need to be told."

BIO: Willow Hill is the cofounder and chief creative officer of Scout Lab, a creative agency building the purpose-driven brands of tomorrow. In her career, she has worked to build brands such as Wix.com, Adidas, Venmo, and more. In addition to running her agency, Willow is on the board of the nonprofit, Many As One. Before starting her company, she spent time building and scaling the Airbnb brand around the globe. Today she also serves as an advisor and angel investor to companies that use emerging technology to solve global issues such as climate change and women's equality.

BRINGING ART TO ADULT ONCOLOGY CENTERS
CONSTANZA ROEDER

"You grieved and dealt with the loss. Now you have the opportunity to create meaning and beauty out of the sorrow."

When Constanza Roeder was diagnosed with leukemia at age 13, everything in her life came to a screeching halt.

"I had all of these ambitious dreams for my future, and then suddenly everything changed," she said. "What I thought my future would look like was no longer a possibility."

Faced with aggressive rounds of chemotherapy, Constanza had to adjust quickly to her new surroundings as a frequent guest at the pediatric oncology wing of her local hospital. The only upside to her hospital stays, she said, were the hospital-sponsored art activities made available to pediatric patients. The arts became her outlet, her escape from sadness, pain, and sickness.

"One of the things that was powerful for me in coping with cancer were the arts because it taught me I could take the raw material of my pain and the trauma I was going through, visualize them and externalize them on a canvas and transform them into whatever I wanted," Constanza said. "Art taught me that I could transcend whatever obstacle I face."

After 130 weeks of chemotherapy, Constanza was officially declared cancer-free. But her battle with cancer had forever left a mark on her psyche and her body. As she got older, Constanza would try to pour her experience into essays, which ultimately translated to scholarships for college. She studied music as an undergraduate.

When she got married and relocated from California to Texas, Constanza decided she wanted to draw upon her childhood experience and volunteer in local adult oncology centers, trying to spread a little cheer and hope to patients. But as she walked the halls of some of the most prestigious medical facilities in the nation, she was shocked by what she found.

"There was no art, nothing on the walls, it was all very drab," Constanza said. "I thought, *oh man, I thought my hospital experience sucked, but this is awful.*"

Though pediatric oncology wings often have art therapy, and visitors like clowns and musical artists to help lift the spirits of the kids, adult oncology patients tend to have a vastly different experience. Constanza realized that while there are hundreds of nonprofits that bring art programs to pediatric oncology units, there are hardly any that cater to adults.

So, she did what she could do in that moment—she started singing. She'd return, week after week, and sing to patients.

"It was as transformative for them as it was for me," Constanza said. "But the thing I heard most from all of the patients is, 'This is great, but we need more.'"

So, she formed a nonprofit called Hearts Need Art: Creative Support for Patients and Caregivers, which would bring music and art therapy to adult oncology patients. For the program to be successful, hospitals would need to work it into their budgets.

"It was then that I started encountering some nos," Constanza said. "There have been several occasions when people have come along and said, 'That's not how that works, you can't do that.'"

Even some hospital executives told her, "This is a great idea, but we don't have the operational budget for it, and we will never have the budget for it."

But Constanza didn't quit. Instead, she created job opportunities and expanded with the help of musicians, painters, poets. Hearts Need Art was formed with a mission to create moments of joy, self-expression, and connection. The results have been extraordinary.

"I had a patient who said, 'We need to remember the reasons why we're alive as much as we need the things that are keeping us alive,'" she recalled. "There are people who need that little bit of light to remember. [They] need moments of joy and self-expression to get through what they're going through."

Hearts Need Art provides both individual one-on-one arts sessions, as well as group sessions in adult oncology centers. Patients can be a little intimidated or shy to begin at first, but as they relax into their creative side, everyone gets into it.

"A lot of people stop using their imagination in childhood because they are told they aren't good at art," Constanza said. "It's tragic because the arts are the languages we have to express our deepest joys and sorrows. When we tell a kid that they can't, that's like saying, 'Oh you're a little bit slow at reading, you must not be talented at this, so we're just not going to teach you to read.' We help people reframe and reclaim the power of their creativity, because they've been told 'no' but we're telling them, 'Yes, yes you can.'"

Although her personal battle with cancer and chemo was harrowing, Constanza is thankful to have gained that perspective from it, because it has primed her to be able to do this current work. She has taken her trauma and turned it into power, helping others when they need it the most.

And the executives from the hospital that told her not to even bother because they'd never find the money? They now have a pending contract. That's the power of never giving up on your dreams.

"There's a level of insight that I bring from my personal experience," she said. "We're all familiar with the five stages of grief, and the end one is acceptance. Well, in the last few years they've talked about adding a sixth level, and that's meaning. You grieved and dealt with the loss. Now you have the opportunity to create meaning and beauty out of the sorrow. That completes the circle. It's been healing for me in my own journey."

BIO: Constanza Roeder is the founder and CEO of Hearts Need Art: Creative Support for Patients and Caregivers. An adolescent leukemia survivor herself, she knows firsthand the power of the arts for healing. She graduated with a degree in vocal performance and minor in psychology from Bethany University and has run her own voice studio business since 2008. Roeder spent many years as a professional musical theater actress and performed in venues around the country. She started as a musician-in-residence at Methodist Hospital in San Antonio in 2010 and founded Hearts Need Art in 2016 to bring more artists and musicians into the hospital. Roeder speaks around the country about the healing power of the arts. She is the recipient of the 2018 Graceann Durr Humanitarian Award and her work has been featured in ThriveGlobal, New York Singing Teachers Association, National Association of Teachers of Singing, News Break, and on the cover of *MD News* magazine.

TOOLS TO TRIUMPH

The Champions featured in this chapter have all been chosen for their ability to use their own life circumstances and experiences to champion for others. When we use our own unique perspective to help lift others up, we tap into our divine purpose and become unstoppable. Whether becoming advocates for at-risk youth or fighting for representation in corporate messaging and branding, these women are making the world a more inclusive and awesome place. Here are the strategies they used when the going got tough.

1. **They stayed close to their "why"**

   Entrepreneurship ain't for the faint of heart. For Adriana Mallozzi, developing a piece of adaptive tech has been a journey full of ups and downs. Some days are exciting and full of possibility, other days it feels like everyone is telling her "no." But Adriana has sustained momentum by remaining focused on her end goal and the outcome. Her work will improve the lives of so many people, and she has never lost sight of *why* she's doing this.

   What are you working on? *Why* is it important that you succeed? What impact are you making? How are you solving a problem or helping others.

2. **They looked for mentors**

   When things were at their worst for Dr. Froswa' Booker-Drew, she sought out mentors who could help. From members of her church to advisors in her school, Froswa' sought out advice when she needed it. She now offers this to others, championing for impoverished communities nearby and instituting a giving circle within her community.

   Where could you seek out mentorship? What communities could you engage with, either in person, or virtually, for help and support?

3. **They worked to make a difference**

   Leslie Pitt took her lived experience with limb loss and created a nonprofit that helps children in developing nations find access to prosthetic limbs. She also wrote a children's book to help tomorrow's generation learn to view others who might look different to them with compassion and excitement.

   What challenges have you lived through? Can you make a difference in someone's life with your learned experience?

4. **They fought for future generations**

   Willow Hill grew up feeling like she just didn't fit in, because she never saw anyone who looked like her. This feeling eventually led her to work in branding, where she plays an integral role in shifting the narrative of giant companies, thus making this world a more inclusive place.

   Can you do something similar? Think about the way you were raised. What can you do to ensure your children, and their children, don't have to go through what you did? What knowledge can you impart? What do you know now that you wish you'd known sooner?

5. **They did work that gave meaning to their struggles**

   Constanza Roeder drew upon her battle with childhood leukemia to make a difference when volunteering with adult oncology patients and refused to believe that her nonprofit couldn't find funding, even when initially told so by hospital executives. Constanza Roeder talks about the sixth stage of grief: meaning.

   All of us will experience loss in this lifetime. How can you give it meaning?

The WARRIORS

Cultivating Inner Fire and Discovering Your Strength

THE WARRIORS WHO OVERCAME "YOU AREN'T STRONG ENOUGH"

"If your heart is broken, make art with the pieces."
—*Shane Koyczan*

The day I pulled out every single one of my eyelashes was as regular as any other. It started with an itch I couldn't seem to scratch, after petting the family cat. When the first lash came out with a satisfying tug, I felt a small sense of relief. With the next three, a little more. Before I knew it, I was pulling out multiple lashes by the root. I rolled them in between my fingers and made wishes by the handful. Ten minutes later and my eyelids were almost completely bald.

It's not so bad, I thought, surveying the damage to my 10-year-old face in the mirror. *I bet no one will even notice.* But the second I found my mother in the kitchen, her hands flew to her mouth in shock.

Uh-oh. My mind scanned for an excuse but came up with nothing. I felt like the world's biggest freak, and now everyone who looked at me would know it.

For the next three weeks I tried not to touch my eyes and willed my lashes to grow back, all the while worrying they never would. I was plagued with regret and shame. Each morning before fourth grade, I used eyeliner to try to fill the empty gaps in my eyelids, hoping it was enough to hide what I had done.

Years later, I'd learn that pulling at your eyelashes, eyebrows or hair is a response to extreme stress—an anxiety disorder known as trichotillomania. Hair pulling was my body's way of processing and relieving stress. Thankfully my lashes did grow back, but I confess that during times of stress, I still struggle. I still have to consciously catch myself and redirect that stress or anxiety before I start to tug.

We are all continually healing, physically and emotionally. Our bodies are fragile and full of limitations. Living in them means that at some point we will all have to confront that fragility. We will all experience what it feels like to break down, and hopefully, what it feels like to heal.

In this chapter, you'll learn how other women have overcome struggles with their health and physical bodies. Through every story, you'll notice a theme: getting to the other side of these challenges takes time and determination, and certainly isn't easy or without pain and discomfort.

From developing personal mantras, to later telling their stories in books and on stages around the world, the brave women in this chapter share their stories of battling cancer, multiple sclerosis, and broken necks to show you what the process of healing has looked like for them.

For many in this section, hearing "you can't" or "you're not strong enough," became an almost daily occurrence on their path to recovery, usually spoken by well-meaning doctors and loved ones. When presented with a bevy of worst-case scenarios and a list of things they probably shouldn't do, these ladies put their lives back together and emerged stronger than ever by tuning into their inner voice and making calculated decisions that fueled their souls and energized their bodies. These are the Warriors.

SHE BECAME A BLACK BELT AT 65, DESPITE BRITTLE BONES
PAMM MCFADDEN

"Tell me I can't do something and I will show you just how it is done."

After four separate battles with cancer, Pamm McFadden was left with brittle bones. She had broken 24 of them just doing everyday activities, and one doctor told her that she could break her femur just from standing. She was told she shouldn't really even leave the house.

But staying home forevermore was simply not an option for this avid adventurer. Pamm knew that life itself was never guaranteed, and she didn't want to waste any more time being afraid of what could happen.

"I waited my whole life to travel without time restrictions," Pamm said. "There was no way I was staying home and not leaving my house ever again. From the time that I was told that to today, I have visited 64 countries, with only five of them being repeats."

She also did something else that doctors scoffed at—she took up kickboxing at age 59. At first, she stayed in the back of the room and just exercised, watching others as they practiced sparring. Slowly, she gained the courage to get out onto the mats herself. It was intimidating at first.

"Eighteen months later I put my white belt on," Pamm said.

"Now I'm sparring with the men, who also take me for granted and just stand there and let me hit them. I had gotten behind one guy's defenses one time and clocked him. Not that I can punch very hard, but he noticed, and he put his hands on his hip and said, 'Miss McFadden, that was awesome!'"

Though doctors had negative opinions about her kickboxing, Pamm was hooked. She set a goal to become a black belt by age 65 and achieved her goal at 64. When she put on that black belt, she beamed with pride. Kickboxing had strengthened more than just her mind and her physical body—it had strengthened her bones as well.

"When I took up kickboxing, all of my doctors laughed," she said. "That was 10 years ago. But kickboxing has given me stronger bones—so much so that my doctor wanted to write a paper on me because I have improved so much."

Throughout her life, when others have tried to impose limitations on her, Pamm has proved them all wrong—from bullies in elementary school to educational advisors in the school system. In high school, her guidance counselor told her that she shouldn't even consider college.

"I was told that I should get a job at McDonald's, and if I was really lucky, I could become a shift supervisor," Pamm said. "But I knew I was destined to go to college."

Using those words as fuel, Pamm became certified to teach K-12 (in math, science, history, and PE), and then went back to school to complete an additional five-year degree in architecture. She established herself as an authority in what was then the niche field of alternative energy: using solar energy to heat and cool a home. She traveled the world lecturing to colleagues about her work, and those travels reignited a passion and a strength within her. Again and again, Pamm beat the odds. Soon she will be going for her second-degree black belt, at 69 years old. And she has no plans of slowing down anytime soon.

"I remember back in high school I was bullied and I was cowed, and I remember being crushed," she said. "But as I was walking home one day, I remember beginning to stand up straighter. It wasn't a 'let me show you,' moment, it was the knowledge within myself that I'm more than that. That's always been with me. That's the red cape in front of me. Tell me I can't do something and I will show you just how it is done."

BIO: Pamm McFadden fell in love with travel when she was about seven years old and her parents drove around the US for a family vacation, and also when she saw TV game shows offering trips as a prize. She was lucky enough to go solo to Northern Ireland at 16, work in France, and then in London. Along the way she used college as an excuse to spend a year studying architecture in Versailles, France, and traveling all over Europe. To this day she still lives by the Leonardo da Vinci quote, "It had long since come to my attention that people of accomplishment rarely sat back and let things happen to them. They went out and happened to things." Next on the list is alligator wrestling. Really. Not kidding. Find her at onlyacarryon.com

FIGHTING THE TABOO SURROUNDING ALOPECIA
EMMA SOTHERN

"Half the power you give your insecurities comes from keeping them to yourself."

Emma Sothern's hair started falling out at age 10. At first her doctors thought it was just stress, caused by the loss of her mother who had recently passed away from the autoimmune disease lupus. But as she got older, the bald spot on her head grew larger.

"I wasn't worried when I found one bald spot, but then it became more of an issue," Emma said. "I was playing sports and I started becoming really self-conscious of my bald spot as it grew."

Emma was diagnosed with alopecia, an autoimmune disorder in which the immune system attacks hair follicles by mistake, causing hair loss. There's no known cure for the disorder. Doctors gave her corticosteroid injections into her head to try and encourage hair growth, to no avail. The youngest of five kids growing up in Ireland, she was naturally shy and demure, and as her bald patch grew, so did her insecurities.

By the time she went to college, she was stuffing these insecurities down with alcohol and substances. When she met her husband two years later, Emma was struggling to come to grips with who she was and the reality that her disorder was presenting.

"By that stage, my hairline was receding faster, and I was really self-conscious of it," she said. "I was wearing stretchy headbands, and I still had big, curly red hair, but I was very self-conscious of the thing, and of my patches."

As her alopecia progressed, Emma began wearing a wig. By this point she was working in advertising and she'd spend up to an hour every morning curling the wig so that it looked like her real hair. Wearing it was supposed to make her feel more confident, but the wig only made her feel worse. Emma constantly felt like she was lying and hiding. She lived in a continual cycle of anxiety of being "found out" by friends or coworkers, which led to stress and even more hair loss. She would come home exhausted from it all.

"I'd come home from work and immediately take off my wig and my husband would always say, 'You look so much better like this, you look so pretty and like yourself,'" she recalled. "I didn't really believe him but the more he said it the more I thought, *Oh, it would be so nice to not have to pretend every day.*"

One day she had just had enough. Ready to be fully herself, Emma asked her husband if he'd shave her head.

"In hindsight it was probably a bit dramatic," Emma said. "But it was a really important thing for me to do."

She drafted a Facebook post, finally talking openly about the battle she had kept hidden for so many years. She included a photo alongside her story. Then she hit "post" with her heart pounding out of her chest.

"It was so empowering," Emma said. "Suddenly all of these people started writing to me about their own struggles with hair loss. And they gave me the push to *keep* writing about it, to keep sharing my own story about it."

Unfortunately, the support she received wasn't universal. A man at her advertising job balked and recoiled when he first saw her bald head.

"One of the guys pulled me aside and said, 'Why did you do this to your head? You could be so attractive, but looking at you, it sickens me. I feel very offended,'" she said. "I didn't know what to do, so I just started apologizing, and I apologized several times, which I'm mad about now of course, because *I* felt bad for *him* feeling offended."

From that point forward Emma decided that other people's opinions weren't going to control her anymore. She decided to take some time to herself, in order to heal and to fully accept her condition. This brought her to spending three months in Indonesia, where she focused on yoga and wellness and decided to see some Eastern medicine healers. Back in Ireland, she found that as her confidence grew, she could speak more freely about living with alopecia and even created her own website on the topic, *Lady Alopecia*.

"Half the power you give your insecurities comes from keeping them to yourself," Emma said. "I used to be so insecure and I cried at everything. Now, my confidence in myself is so much greater. I used to be quite introverted, but now I actually love to wear costumes and fancy dress, and decorate my head with feathers and glitter, and it's brought me closer to this inner diva I never knew I had."

BIO: Emma Sothern, AKA Lady Alopecia, is a freelance copywriter, part-time yoga teacher, and full-time alopecian. Since shaving her remaining hair off at 28, she's never been happier. Now her goal is to help other women—and men—feel confident in their own skin, just as they are! Emma believes the things we're most insecure are actually what make us most interesting. And that sharing these insecurities with others gives us power. Emma's currently working on her memoir, *Becoming Lady Alopecia*, and lives with her lovely (big-bearded, very hairy!) husband in Hoi An, Vietnam. She is a firm believer in color therapy and is mildly obsessed with yellow.

MULTIPLE SCLEROSIS WON'T SLOW HER DOWN
ANGELA BRADFORD

"If life were easy, what would you have to share with anyone?"

When Angela Bradford was seven years old, she made a promise to herself: when she grew up, she was going to be able to afford whatever she wanted.

"I was seven and we were so broke," Angela said. "My mom was trying to homeschool me and my brother, and I didn't realize how broke we were until I said, 'We should buy oranges,' and was told, 'We can't afford oranges.' It finally clicked in my little brain that we were broke and I started bawling."

That was a defining moment for Angela, who told herself right then and there that she'd do whatever it took—even if that meant working three, four, or five jobs if she had to when she was older—

to never worry about income. As soon as she could legally work, she set out to make that a reality. She's since become an expert in reinventing her career however and whenever she sees fit, no matter what anyone else says or thinks about it. Her determination has taken her through many industries, from long-distance truck driving to financial planning, and into her most recent challenge: her diagnosis with multiple sclerosis.

At 18, Angela left her hometown in Alberta, Canada, and went off to be a horse trainer. Everyone around her told her it was a pipe dream, but Angela was good with horses, and the job paid well. When she grew tired of horse training, she made another big leap: to long-distance truck driving.

"Becoming a truck driver was another thing people told me I couldn't do," Angela said. "A girl on the road? Running the highway, in between states? That's not safe, they'd say. You shouldn't do that."

She got her commercial driver's license at the age of 19 and was driving internationally between Canada and the United States by age 21. She might have gotten some strange looks from truckers at truck stops, but she loved the open road.

Though everyone told her it was dangerous, she found it to be just the opposite. Other drivers looked out for her, protected her and kept her safe. Truck driving also helped her make close to a six-figure salary and allowed her to travel more. But the work began to get boring and the long hours draining. Just as Angela was thinking about making another career switch, her beloved dog and road companion got sick.

"I had to put her down, my best friend of thirteen years, in Helena, Montana," she said. "And I knew it was a gift to help me get out of trucking."

It was as good of a time as any to explore another industry, and Angela had been introduced to financial planning and wealth management. Again, the people around her told her they "didn't see it," as a path for her.

"My mother would say things like, 'You've always been blue

collar, I don't see you working in an office,'" she said. "But now they're my biggest fans."

When you have an attitude of certainty that you will succeed, no matter what, you become unstoppable. Angela put this belief into action and is now running a team that has spread across Canada and now into the U.S., with the goal of creating an office in every state and province in the next 15 years.

She's surpassed all of her financial goals, personally and professionally. Her house is paid off in full, she's completely debt-free, and able to invest however she likes. She's a long way from being the little girl asking for oranges. Now she encourages and supports others, especially women, in finding financial freedom and is passionate about teaching her clients how to leverage what they have to generate wealth. Managing money is so important, she says, because you never know what life is going to throw at you.

Last year, Angela was diagnosed with multiple sclerosis. The disease causes the deterioration of your body's muscles and functions. Eventually, it can progress to loss of muscle function, loss of vision, and death. But Angela has always believed that her outlook, grit, and determination can carry her through any obstacle—and this is no exception. She has remained positive and upbeat. Even when MS forced her to walk with a cane. Even when it made her hands numb, making typing difficult.

"Since MS, my mindset has completely shifted," Angela said. "People always ask me, 'Why are you so positive all the time?' But every challenge makes an impact, and I realized that to have a big effect, you have to use your challenges. That's what makes the impact. If life were easy, what would you have to share with anyone?"

BIO: Angela Bradford is a senior marketing director with World Financial Group. Within four years of transitioning from the blue-collar world of trucking and training horses, to the white-collar world of finances and training people, she has opened multiple offices and started expansion into two countries. She has an amazing team working with her and has the goal of opening an office in every state and province in North America within the next 10-15 years.

taunted her for walking around her small island town in heels. They called her a "dreamer" and told her that she had her "head in the clouds" because she preferred to be reading and writing poetry, painting, or playing music rather than hang around with them.

Olga Maria did have dreams—big dreams. She refused to listen to any of the naysayers and instead followed the voice inside of her telling her that she was meant for more.

"I look at it like this: I thank those people who made fun of me, or discouraged my dreams, because they made me stronger as a woman and that made me the woman that I am today," she said.

After high school, Olga Maria decided it was time to make those dreams a reality. She moved from Puerto Rico to Miami and then to New York City, arriving in the city exhausted and exhilarated. It had always been her goal to get back to New York City, having been born in Brooklyn. But arriving in the city so far away from her family and not speaking English was harder than she imagined it would be.

"When I got to New York, some members of my family and other acquaintances back home were saying, 'Oh, she's going to come back crying in a few months, she can't speak English, she doesn't know anyone in New York,'" she said. "I had to start from zero and work two to three jobs, while also taking [English as a second language] classes."

It certainly wasn't easy at first. She failed several of her initial ESL tests. She'd cry in frustration after studying so hard, only to get her tests back covered in red ink. But she never gave up trying to learn and practiced speaking English as often as she could.

"I remember a professor I met who changed my life," Olga Maria said. "He said, 'You can always learn grammar, but you can't ever learn perspective. You have a very interesting perspective.'"

It was then that Olga Maria realized her greatest insecurities could also be the key to her greatest power. People were always asking her why she was running all over New York City in heels, so she decided to embrace this, and started a travel blog in 2013 that she named *Dreams in Heels*.

"My brand started through me wanting to take something negative, and turning it into something positive," she said. "I want to help empower women to feel comfortable in whatever shoes they choose."

Dreams in Heels grew steadily and quickly, and is now one of the top resources for solo female and adventure travelers. Olga Maria has been featured in *Forbes* and has won awards from companies like Mastercard and *Latina* magazine, who named her a "Next Generation Latina" in 2012. In 2016, she also founded the first and largest community for Latina travelers on Facebook, called Latinas Who Travel, which was created to inspire and empower more Latinas to get out of their comfort zone and to travel on their own terms.

Olga Maria has traveled the world and has had experiences she once only dreamed of, but initially, she was nervous to share more of her personal story with her community.

"In the beginning, I thought people would see me as a victim," she said. "But they told me, 'No, we see you as an inspiration.'"

She's come a long way from being that young girl in braces and boots. These days she's wandering the world the way she always dreamed she would.

"It's unbelievable," she said. "I never thought a small-town girl like me could travel the world and work with the companies I get to work with now, all in hopes of inspiring the next generation of Latinas, people who identify and see themselves in me. For me, that is one of the most meaningful parts of what I do."

BIO: Olga Maria Czarkowski is a professional travel writer, storyteller and a full-time digital nomad who runs an award-winning solo female travel and lifestyle blog called *Dreams in Heels*. Her blog features travel and style tips, trending destinations and off-the-beaten-path recommendations to inspire people (especially women) to follow their dreams. She is also the founder of the bilingual (Spanish/English) travel community, Latinas Who Travel, a community where Latinas are encouraged to share their journeys, since during her extensive travels (around Europe, Asia, Africa, the Middle East, Latin America, the Caribbean, USA, and Canada) Olga did not meet many other Latinas. Olga also loves sharing her expertise, tips and story to inspire others, and has been featured in publications and on sites such *Forbes*, POPSUGAR, Matador Network, Huffington Post, Univision, Telemundo, *Latina* magazine, and many others. She is also a global speaker, the travel editor of *Livid* magazine and has been featured as a travel ambassador on video series with Hiplatina.com and Belatina.com.

LIVING LIFE 2.0, AFTER AN ACCIDENT BROKE HER NECK
HEIDI SIEFKAS

"We don't have much control over these things that happen in life, whether that's freak accidents, pandemics or politics. But we do have a way to shift the perspective."

Heidi Siefkas was living what she *thought* was her dream life. She was happily married, climbing up the ladder in her career, living in a house that had more bathrooms than people. She had everything she had ever wanted and things were just about perfect, she thought. But then one day, the unimaginable happened.

"I did something that everybody does," Heidi said. "I ordered a pizza, because I didn't want to cook, and my husband who was an executive chef didn't want to cook. The next morning, I was taking out the pizza box to the dumpster, and the next thing I recall, I was waking up in the trauma unit of the ICU."

On an otherwise ordinary autumn day, a 1,000-lb. tree limb had come crashing down upon her in her front yard, breaking her neck instantly and leaving her unconscious. A bystander called for help.

"There comes a point in time, and this happens for everyone in life, when you're just juggling: one ball, two balls, and you're waiting for the next ball to drop," Heidi said. "Needless to say, all of those balls in my life dropped in that moment, because my life was put on a forced pause."

In the aftermath of this freak accident, everything about her life as she knew it would change. The tree limb broke her C7, the vertebra responsible for the mobility of her hands and eyes, she said. She underwent neurosurgery and many months of rehabilitation, which included at least six months of being more or less immobile, so that her vertebrae could naturally fuse. Heidi was lucky to be alive, but the accident had changed absolutely everything about her life.

"The ripple effect of this one-thousand-pound tree limb was seen in every aspect of my life," she said. "The happy marriage? That was a facade. Many of those things that I thought formed my identity were changed."

During the six months of her recovery in which she was mostly bedridden and had to be sponge-bathed by someone else, Heidi uncovered a trail of deception in her marriage. Her husband had been living a double life with someone else for over a year. She was devastated, and the hits felt like they just kept on coming.

Soon after, her job told her that they could no longer wait for her to return, and Heidi was forced to resign. When she was cleared to stand out of bed again, she found that her muscles had atrophied and no longer knew how to support her body.

"Not only was my own body different, but my identity as a wife, and as a professional, was flipped on its back," she said. "Absolutely everything had been turned upside down. But the gift in all of this was the forced pause."

With everything gone, Heidi had the rare opportunity of space and time: she had nothing to do but reflect on what was no longer working in her life and imagine what could be.

"I had an opportunity, once I got my wits about me, to rebuild my former life, or to decide to use this low point as a springboard for positive growth to do what I didn't know I wanted to do previously," she said.

In that moment she realized that she was totally burnt out from working so many years in public relations and marketing. She also understood that however painful a breakup might be, she could not continue in her marriage. In the wake of all of this, she had a chance to do life over. Life 2.0, she called it.

"I said to myself, 'Alright, you're going to be the architect of this life,'" Heidi said. "You're going to build it from scratch, and you might not bring anything from that former life back into this. So, in essence, I literally and figuratively threw out the trash that day."

One by one, she made difficult decisions. She moved forward with a divorce, and with selling their home. She had worked for years on the public relations side of the travel industry, but now the cubicle life no longer appealed to her. She wanted to be out experiencing the world again.

"Before I went back to the workforce, I wanted to do something that would test myself wholly," Heidi said. "So I decided to do a walkabout. I went to the southernmost tip of Patagonia, Chile, and went on a three-week life test where I physically tested myself by doing the W Trek in the Torres del Paine National Park."

The contrast of turquoise blues, glaciers, and granite towers gave life to her transformation. As she traveled from the bottom of the Strait of Magellan all the way up to Santiago, Chile, and over to Buenos Aires, Argentina, she made new friends and shared with them more about her story using her second language, Spanish. She had a deep understanding that she was on the right path.

"I knew then that I was healthy enough, that I was okay on my own, and perhaps that I had another relationship in me, that I had the opportunity to love again," she said.

She also understood that her story was powerful. When she returned to the United States, she decided it was time to write a book. In 2014, she released her first book, *When All Balls Drop: The Upside to Losing Everything.*

"I always tell people that we don't have much control over these things that happen in life, whether that's freak accidents, pandemics or politics," Heidi said. "But we do have a way to shift the perspective."

Since the accident, Heidi has adopted a mantra: "Look Up." Be in the moment, absorbing life and all of its beauty, and find the positive in any situation.

"Just about anyone that we admire has often had a humdinger of a low point, but they've used it as a springboard," she said. "'Look Up' really embodies what I'd like to educate the world about, and that's post-traumatic growth. There is a silver lining to almost any terrible situation in life."

Today, Heidi lives in Maui, Hawaii, practicing "Look Up" and aloha. She is also the author of three books and is a motivational speaker who has shared her story on the TEDx stage.

"Don't wait for a tree to fall on you to realize that you're not as happy in life as you could be," Heidi said. "Go out, and live life the way you want to, today. Right now. I'm a big believer in adventure. I tell people to embrace adventure, and to do it frequently. Challenge yourself to get out of the norm. Getting out of the norm is what makes you look at things differently. It flips the switch."

BIO: Heidi Siefkas is an award-winning author, TEDx speaker, and adventurer. Originally from Galesville, Wisconsin, Heidi now lives in Maui, Hawaii. However, as an adventurer, Heidi is rarely home for very long. The author of three inspirational non-fiction books, *When All Balls Drop*, *With New Eyes*, and *Cubicle to Cuba*, she has created the mantra "Look Up" and speaks to groups worldwide. You can connect with her at heidisiefkas.com.

TOOLS TO TRIUMPH

One of my best friends got into a horrific car accident as I was writing this book. She broke her pelvis, sacrum, several vertebrae in her back and neck, her clavicle, and her ankle. She lacerated her spleen, bladder, kidney, and adrenal gland. She was pulled from a burning car by a stranger named Jesus in the middle of the night, lost deep in the back roads of the Arizona desert. It is a miracle that she is alive.

Tragedies happen each and every day. When everything goes wrong, what pushes a person to continue living life on their terms, post-healing? The brave Warriors in this section have collectively faced a variety of accidents and illnesses. Here are some specific strategies they employed to get through their most trying times.

1. **They invested time and energy into new hobbies and passions**

   When Pamm McFadden was told she shouldn't leave her house because her bones were too brittle, she simply refused to entertain that idea. Instead, she invested her time and energy into a new hobby, kickboxing. Martial arts gave her mind a still place to return to, a space where she could channel emotion.

   If everything around you just sort of blows, what can you pour your time and energy into that makes you feel good? What can you do that's just for you? Are you interested in learning a new language? Developing a meditation practice? Doing yoga? Swimming laps? Give your brain and body a place to go to find stillness.

2. **They built a supportive community where there was none previously**

   Battling alopecia was a private struggle for Emma Sothern, until the day she decided to talk about it publicly with her friends and family on Facebook. She had no idea that her share that day would invite others to also disclose their own struggles with hair loss. Nor did she realize at the time that she would go on to build a large community in this space.

   You just don't know how your story may impact someone else. What sort of a community do you wish had existed when you were at your lowest? Can you create that? How can you share your story in hopes of inspiring others?

3. **They focused on the positives**

Angela Bradford is consistently asked by other people how she stays so positive despite her MS diagnosis. She knows that life has ups and downs, but she chooses to focus on the positives of any situation. With this mindset, she's been able to tackle even the steepest of challenges.

If life were easy, she reminds us, what stories and lessons would we have to share with one another? Can you do the same? Can you find the silver lining to a difficult situation you've encountered?

4. **They embraced their insecurities as strengths**

I have never met a single person on this Earth who isn't insecure about something. Whether it's weight, or height, skin, breath, or feet, we all have something going on that we wish were different. But what if we looked at these insecurities as teachers, and our fears as the fabric for building a community? When Olga Maria Czarkowski was growing up with a shortened Achilles tendon, the kids teased her and called her "Robocop." In sharing some of these painful memories, she found a community who embraced her and an inner strength she didn't know she had.

What are your biggest insecurities? Can you see the liberation and the power you might feel in sharing them? How many people you might inspire that you would not have otherwise? Don't deprive the world of your unique perspective and gifts.

5. **They reinvented themselves in the wake of tragedy**

When a tree limb came crashing down on Heidi Siefkas, her entire life as she knew it changed. In the wake of everything she lost, she was forced to make a choice: try to rebuild things the way they were, or, become the architect of a new life. She began by thinking about the things that brought her joy, and the things she always wanted to do. Little by little, she created a new lifestyle full of adventure, travel, and joy. Experts have found that setting mini goals can be beneficial in the wake of tragedy. For Heidi, these small goals started out small and grew larger. "Just take one step" became, "Just walk to the end of the hall," which turned into hiking in Torres del Paine. Day-by-day. Step-by-step. Can you relate?

The TRAILBLAZERS

Rewriting the Rules—Becoming Unstoppable

THE TRAILBLAZERS WHO OVERCAME
"YOU CAN'T DO THAT"

> *"Do not judge me by my success, judge me by how many times I fell down and got back up again."*
> —*Nelson Mandela*

On a cold December night in 2010, I had a dream in which I was staring at a hot-pink travel guidebook made just for women. I could see it all—the brand name, the colors, the content. I kept thinking *you should've done this, this was totally your calling!*

At the time, I was working as a journalist for a trade publication and nothing about my work made me feel proud. I was regurgitating ad copy and trying to pretend like it was editorial and newsworthy to satisfy a corporate client. I came home every day demoralized and with eyes bloodshot. My soul was nagging at me to get back to traveling and living abroad, something I had been doing years prior that defined so much of my identity and happiness.

Halfway through my next workday, I sat at my desk under the obnoxiously bright fluorescent lights, killing time between assignments. Suddenly, the idea came flooding back to me. Excitement flowed through my body as I typed "travel guidebooks for women," into Google, waiting for results to tell me someone else had already created the idea.

By 2010, the Internet was already a pretty happening place. I figured there was no way that this idea hadn't been created yet, but pages of digging turned nothing up.

There was no "women's travel industry" that I could find. There were no "women's travel guidebooks," and only a few blogs that had content specific to solo female travel.

"How is this possible?" I asked myself. Instantly a thought popped into my head: *So that you could create it.*

Suddenly I knew this idea was divine, that it was mine for a reason, and that I had to start it—now. Never mind the fact that I had zero experience in writing or publishing guidebooks. It was my obligation to see this vision through.

I made a promise to the idea itself, right then. I would do anything to make it a reality—from sleeping on other people's couches to living on cans of tuna fish when I ran out of money (all things that happened)—if it would just remain mine for a while longer until I could actualize it.

Three months later, I was in Thailand writing what would become the first in a series of destination-specific guidebooks for women. Quitting my awful editorial job meant that suddenly I got to make all the decisions: what properties to feature in our pages and the criteria by which to select them. What insider info to pass onto our reader. Even what the weight of the page should feel like.

I had the chance to fully reimagine the guidebook industry. What did I want it to look like? How could I remake it to be more inclusive and applicable to the experience of solo female travelers? I started writing down travel tips that my girlfriends and I would share with one another that I couldn't find in other guidebooks.

Things like which bus station was kind of sketchy at night, and which cities you couldn't find tampons in.

Of course, I met people—usually men—who tried to question and dissuade me. They'd say things like:

> *"Do women even need their own guidebooks?"*
> *"If this could make money, wouldn't Lonely Planet have thought of it already?"*
> *"You'll never be able to make any money with guidebooks."*

I didn't listen. Go! Girl Guides became the world's first series of travel guidebooks for women, publishing seven guidebooks for women (and counting), while producing over 2k pages of blog content created by a team of more than 30 writers and editors. The business has been featured in publications like the *New York Times*, CNN, and *Forbes*.

In the process of following this dream, I myself became a Trailblazer: a leader in an industry that hadn't quite yet developed (women's travel), which has since exploded. One prominent media outlet even referred to me as: "The woman making travel better (and safer) for all women." Wowza. I couldn't have seen that coming!

If I had waited for someone to give me permission—or worse, if I had listened to the naysayers who questioned the idea and my ability to be the person who could create it—I would've missed the boat completely and probably lost interest in the idea altogether.

The Trailblazers in this section are all women who have taken swift action to actualize their dreams, and who gave *themselves* permission to do, be, or create. When all they found were closed doors and a world trying to tell them that they "can't be/dream/do that," these powerhouses kicked down those doors and reinvented themselves and their industries. They defined their own path, paving the way for others to follow their trail. These are the Trailblazers.

BUILDING A BEAUTIFUL, SUCCESSFUL LIFE AFTER 60
SANDRA HART

"The secret ingredient is believing you're worthy and that you deserve."

Sandra Hart has been proving the naysayers wrong her whole life. Now the host of the popular YouTube channel, *Life Over Sixty With Sandra* – a channel she launched at age 79 – she encourages women to live their fullest lives at any age, despite anyone who tries to tell them that they can't.

Part of the inspiration behind her series comes from Sandra's own life experiences. As the former host of *Romper Room* and an actress who found success after the age of 50, there have been many people along her journey who have tried to tell her what she was and wasn't capable of—and she has proved them wrong, time and time again.

Raised in a small, industrial town in Ohio, Sandra couldn't wait to get out and experience the world.

"When I was 18, I said goodbye to my family and went to college, and I remember as I flew away and saw their figures getting smaller and smaller, I said, 'Sayonara, I am never coming back,' and I never really did," Sandra recalled.

College wasn't even really her dream. Sandra always wanted to be an actress, but her father had forbidden it. So off to college she went, where she met a man that she'd go on to marry and have two children with. It was what everyone else was doing, too.

"My dreams just kind of slid down the tube," she said. "I didn't have a life and I was living his life instead."

When that marriage ended, Sandra had to figure out how to support two little kids. One day, she spotted an ad for a television host and felt her intuition ping. She was certain she had to apply.

"I didn't have any of the qualifications they were looking for," Sandra said. "I wasn't a teacher, I had nothing they had said they wanted except that I was a woman. I thought *well, there's nothing they can say but no.*"

She shuffled into the audition, surrounded by young, pretty, ambitious girls who had backgrounds in show business and certainly had more of the qualifications the producers said they were looking for in the ad. It was the 1960s, and Sandra was older than nearly everyone in the room and felt a little bit nervous about that. But, she figured, she had nothing to lose. "I said to myself, 'There's a reason I'm here,'" Sandra recalled.

She was right. Over 250 applicants auditioned, but Sandra won the job and became the Baltimore-based *Romper Room* host known as "Miss Sandra."

She was finally in front of the camera, where she always knew she belonged. It was the start of a career that Sandra would return to again and again, moving from *Romper Room* in 1970 to a position as a news anchor for a CBS affiliate. Things were going great professionally, but at home, things had become chaotic.

Sandra had remarried, and had another child, a son. But her husband was suffering from undiagnosed schizophrenia, which manifested itself in abuse, fear, and constant accusations. Things got physically violent at times. One night, he lunged at her with a screwdriver, accusing her of being unfaithful. Fortunately, she was able to knock him off balance and quickly flee with the children. She filed for divorce.

Though these dark days were difficult to endure, Sandra knew that she couldn't let them define her. She had young children for whom she needed to provide and set an example. She had dreams that she still wanted to pursue.

"That gave me the opportunity to do what I had always wanted to do, and what my father denied me, and that was to be an actress," Sandra said. "I was 50 years old and I said to myself, 'I can because I want it. It's my dream, and I'm going to go for it.'"

She jumped in fully. Sandra got her Screen Actors Guild (SAG) card, and before she knew it, began landing lead roles in off-Broadway plays, as well as roles in television shows like *Law and Order*. She worked with directors like Martin Scorsese and Woody Allen. She created a beautiful life for herself, made all the more lovely by the fact that she was finally following her heart.

At age 79, Sandra decided she wasn't done yet. So, she started a YouTube channel encouraging women over age 60 to live their biggest and best lives. At age 81, she received notice that her channel had grown to over 2.5 million views.

"There's a freedom to life over 60, and it's not a curse like some women used to believe," she said. "You're never too old to open another chapter, never too old to start writing, painting, taking voice lessons. The secret ingredient is believing you're worthy and that you deserve it. That this is your dream, this what you want to do, and you know that you're a worthy person. That's what I want to instill in every single woman who crosses my path."

BIO: Sandra Hart is a YouTube influencer with her channel *Life Over 60 With Sandra*. She is a former *Romper Room* teacher, an actress, author, lifestyle blogger, and a certified life coach. Sandra's goal is to live a life of purpose.

📺 http://bit.ly/2AnESPs

📷 @sandrashart

📖 Books: https://tinyurl.com/yxqb4ycz

THIS ATHLETE IS CHALLENGING
FITNESS STEREOTYPES
MIRNA VALERIO

*"Your body is incredible and it can
do really awesome things, if you
let it. If you allow yourself to do
those awesome things and believe
in its awesomeness."*

Mirna Valerio was going about her business, juggling her busy life as a mother and teacher, when out of nowhere her heart started racing.

"I thought I was having a heart attack," Mirna said. "After eight hours of testing, they decided it was a panic attack. So, I was sitting there on the hospital table trying to figure out why I would be having a panic attack?"

Nothing was happening in her life that was more stressful than usual, per se, but Mirna realized she had been treading water for a long time, prioritizing the demands of her work as an educator and the needs of her family over her own.

"Everything was about work and family, and not necessarily in that order," she said. "Sometimes it was family then work, sometimes it was work then family, but it was never me. I was never in that mix."

The doctor delivered some terrifying words: "If you want to see your son grow up, you're going to have to change your lifestyle."

Mirna had always loved the outdoors. As a kid growing up in Brooklyn, New York, she'd often spend time with her family camping or at summer camps. She had also always loved to run. At the doctor's office, she realized she needed to make a change. The way she had been living wore her into the ground. She had put on weight and become less active. If she wanted a brighter future, she was going to have to slow down, get moving, and revisit the things that had brought her joy earlier in life.

"That was a series of cathartic moments for me where I realized I needed to redo things and prioritize my life," she said. "And I did. I started running again."

She started off small, getting on the treadmill and running just one mile. Once she refamiliarized her body with what it felt like to run a mile, she started setting bigger goals. One mile turned into two, which turned into a 5k. Her colleagues at the boarding school where she worked suggested training together. Pretty soon 5ks turned into 10ks, which turned into half-marathons.

"I discovered pure grit within me," Mirna said. "To run a marathon is really hard. It's hard on your body; it's hard on your social life, because all you're doing is running or sleeping or eating. But I loved it. I loved how it made me feel."

Returning to running also fueled her with new energy. She started a blog called *Fat Girl Running* to share more about her journey to health and wellness.

"I wanted to share what it was like when I was running these long distances and most people did not look like me, mainly in body size," she said. "I also was running mostly on trails, and you didn't see a lot of Black people there either."

Mirna told stories on her blog about training for the marathon, recovering from injuries, and that one time she lied to her friends about how far they were really running. She also shared about how people seemed to perceive her while running.

"Lots of people were super positive and friendly, but then there were other people who were like, 'What are you doing out here?'" Mirna said. "Or they'd say things like, 'Maybe you should walk, you'll lose more weight that way.' Those kinds of comments were super common, along with the positive and encouraging ones, and the overly encouraging ones like, 'Oh my god, good for you!' Those types of things—where people really are astonished that you're out there doing a thing that your body is supposed to do anyway, that your body is meant to be doing. Really in their head, they're thinking only a certain type of body should be out there doing that."

One night, Mirna found herself in a mood. Her back was hurting, the week had been stressful, and she was tired of doctors telling her to "try dieting" without fully understanding that she was an athlete running five to seven times a week, focusing on long-term health and wellness. She turned to her keyboard and let it all out.

"I had this negative circuit of thoughts going in my head, thinking of all the negative things people had told me," she said. "And that blog post, it didn't go viral, but I had never seen that many people sharing and commenting before."

That one post changed everything. The next week, a reporter from the *Wall Street Journal* called and asked her for an interview. That interview turned into another with *Runner's World*, who did a 12-page spread on her.

"I was like 'What is happening here?'" she said. "I'm just trying to run, this is crazy."

But it never slowed down. In sharing her story and helping to shatter the myth that being "fit" looks a certain way, Mirna created an entirely new career. She appeared in ads for Calvin Klein. She shot commercials for major brands. And she did most of this, while still holding onto her teaching job. The staff at the school where she was teaching were incredibly supportive of her along the way, but soon enough, Mirna had to make a choice.

"It was the end of 2017, around Christmas, and it was a tipping point," she said. "I had just traveled to Boston to shoot a J.C. Penney commercial and the check that I got was a quarter of my teaching salary, and I made it in seven hours. So, I said to my husband, 'I'm not going to sign my (teaching) contract for next year. I'm doing this thing and it hasn't stopped. It's been almost three years, so I think I can do it.' He said, 'Can you do other things?' I said, 'Do you even know me? Have we been married 17 years? I do a lot of things. I have always done a lot of things.' That was really disappointing to me."

The universe shows us what's possible for each of us, but it's up to us to walk through those doors. Though it was scary to let go of her work as an educator, when Mirna made the decision to become a full-time athlete and an influencer, that pivotal decision ushered in a whole new wave of abundance.

She released her first book, *A Beautiful Work in Progress*, which became a bestseller. She has traveled the world speaking at conferences and leading retreats. She still does a fair amount of teaching and educating, these days about anti-racism. She's living life, by design.

"The body is incredible," Mirna said. "That's the message I want to get through to people. Your body is incredible and it can do really awesome things, if you let it. If you allow yourself to do those awesome things and believe in its awesomeness. Other people might not. But that's their own darkness and their own limited views and you don't need those people in your life. Just do you."

BIO: Mirna Valerio is a native of Brooklyn, New York, and is a former educator, now a cross-country coach, ultrarunner, obstacle course enthusiast, and author of the recently published memoir, *A Beautiful Work in Progress*. Although she began running in high school, she recommitted to the sport after a health scare in 2008. It was then that her love for running and all its attendant benefits were reignited. She soon started her blog *Fat Girl Running*, about her experiences as a larger woman in a world of thinner athletes. Mirna's athletic story was featured in the *WSJ*, *Runner's World*, on the NBC Nightly News, CNN, on the CW Network, and in the viral REI-produced documentary short, *The Mirnavator*. Her writing has been featured in *Women's Running* magazine, Self Magazine Online, Outside Online, and *Runner's World* magazine. Most recently, she was chosen as a 2018 National Geographic Adventurer of the Year.

AFTER BEING TYPECAST IN HOLLYWOOD, SHE WROTE HER OWN ROLES

LUCIANA FAULHABER

"You said I couldn't do it, so I wrote it myself."

Luciana Faulhaber has always been lovingly referred to by her family as "the stubborn one." The youngest of four children, raised by a single mother in a modest home in Rio de Janeiro, Brazil, her mom often joked with the future scientist-turned-actress and producer about how determined a person she was, even from birth.

"She jokes that I'm so stubborn that nothing can really stop me," Luciana said. "She said, 'Not even birth control could keep you from being born.' So when I'm feeling discouraged, I think of this story."

Since she was a little girl, Luciana had dreamed of becoming an actress. The family didn't have cable growing up, but they did have a collection of classic movies. Late at night, with the television on mute, she would tip-toe across the living room to watch Fred Astaire dance across her screen. She loved the feeling these films gave her, how they made her feel powerful and glamorous and limitless.

"When I got old enough to voice this to my mom, to say, 'I want to be an actor,' her immediate response was, 'No, you can't,'" Luciana said. "How are you going to pay for your survival? She would say, 'The arts are for the rich.'"

But Luciana wouldn't let it go, so as a compromise, her mother allowed her to go to acting classes if she got good grades in school.

The arts were always treated as a reward, but never a career path. Books became her other escape.

Though acting was her primary dream, Luciana also had a fascination with science. When she decided to apply to study in the United States for college, she didn't just aim for one school, she applied to *all* of the top colleges in New York City, including Fordham University, New York University, and Columbia University—and was accepted to them all.

Fordham offered her a scholarship, so she enrolled and picked up three jobs to pay for her living expenses. She babysat by night and studied biology by day. It was the American dream, except for one problem: her college advisor wasn't exactly supportive of her academic goals.

"My college advisor was one of the first people who told me I couldn't do something because I was an immigrant," she said. "At the time I wanted to be a biology major because I always loved science. But (Fordham) was a liberal arts school and he said, 'No, your first language is not English, so you can't be a science major.' I said, 'That's funny, because scientists work in Latin so that they can collaborate and share findings across languages.'"

The two continued to spar throughout her time in school, sometimes getting into full verbal arguments in his office, with his office door wide open. Nonetheless, she graduated with a dual degree in teaching and in science, and that same advisor ended up writing her a recommendation for her graduate studies at Columbia University. It said:

> *"Loves to stand up against authority, has a mind of her own, tends not to follow directions when strategically given, finds her own way to do things."*

When you're meant to do something in life, that thing has a way of finding you. Though Luciana had fought hard for her degree and found a position teaching special education and science in an elementary school in New York City, it wasn't what she felt she was meant to be doing. One day, while she was standing in front of her class, the universe intervened.

"I was teaching in my classroom at the school, and this man walks by," Luciana recalled. "Then he walks by again. And finally, he comes into my classroom and says, 'Hey, would you ever be interested in being in a commercial? I'm a casting director for commercials, and my kid goes to this school and every year I do a commercial and I bring teachers in.'"

Luciana said yes and went to the school's auditorium to record a casting tape. But when she asked the school principal for a day off from work for the opportunity, she was told she couldn't have it. It was the first time Luciana had to choose between work in the entertainment industry, which was her dream, or her traditional teaching career.

It was her fork in the road moment, but an easy decision. She called in sick to her teaching job, went to the gig, and with that, became an actress in the union.

Before long, she was working full time as an actress. She relocated to Los Angeles to pursue her dream, but soon came in contact with all of the darker sides of Hollywood. It was 2012, long before the Me Too movement would call for greater accountability and protections. She came across sleazy industry men who used their positions to sexually harass her. Many of the roles she was auditioning for as a Latinx actress were written stereotypically, so she found herself auditioning again and again for roles like, "prostitute," "drug dealer's girlfriend," or "nurse."

"I auditioned for twenty nurse roles, but never a doctor," she said. "I kept complaining, saying, 'I want to audition for the main role, why can't I? And I kept getting, 'No, they're looking for this type.' So I said, 'Fuck this, I'm going to create my own work.'"

That's how Luciana became a producer. She began with a play, teaming up with a friend to pull it off. It did well. Her next project was a low-budget horror film, in which she also played the lead role. Some people said, "That's not how things are done in Hollywood," or, "You don't know anything about producing films," or, "You won't be able to afford it."

But at every pass, Luciana found a way to make her dreams a reality, whether that meant crowdfunding a project or pushing it in front of the right champion. With this mentality, she found success.

She's appeared on shows such as *Grey's Anatomy* and *CSI*, and in movies like *Iron Man 3*. She's currently working on producing a documentary. She's produced socially conscious films about topics like femicide and homelessness, and she's just getting started.

"I'm really proud that I made something that was different from other things I have seen, and that I could get the part that they said I couldn't play," she said. "You said I couldn't do it, so I wrote it myself."

BIO: Luciana Faulhaber is a first-generation Latinx immigrant. The first of her family to attend graduate school, she dedicated her time to combining her studies in international development at Columbia University with her passion for filmmaking as a vehicle for shining a light on political issues, with the goal of making a social impact. She founded "Enuff" (Enough) Productions with Javier E. Gomez, with the intent to create opportunities for people of color in front of and behind the camera. Luciana has created projects that discuss immigration, racism, and homelessness, and is now developing a documentary addressing the issues of women's rights and sexual liberation, the civil rights movement, and equality. She has also received accolades for her feature film directorial debut, with *Don't Look* being nominated for Best Director (North Hollywood Film Festival and Crimson Screen), and Best Picture (Crimson Screen), winning six awards including the Spotlight Silver Award for Innovation in Independent Filmmaking. As an actress, you can see her work in *Shades of Blue*, *Grey's Anatomy*, and *Iron Man 3* among others.

SHE QUIT BUZZFEED TO MODEL, AND IS TOTALLY SLAYING
JARRY LEE

"What I learned was to focus on standing out, rather than on trying to fit in."

Jarry Lee had been working as a deputy editor for BuzzFeed for four years when she realized she just wasn't happy in what she had thought was her dream job.

Growing up in Wales, her goal had always been to work with books and publishing, and here she was, just a couple of years out of college, working as the books and culture editor for one of the largest and most well-known companies in the world. But something just didn't *feel* right.

So, she let herself dream. If she could do anything, what would she do? She remembered how in school she had always had so much fun in acting classes.

"I figured, why not see what that looks like?" Jarry said. "I made some profiles and headshots for acting, and it was really fun."

But acting is competitive, and she also wanted to explore modeling. In meeting with different modeling agencies, several directors told her that she wouldn't be able to book jobs with her blonde hair, and that she should dye it black for more of a "traditional Asian" look. But Jarry uses her hair as a form of expression, so she said, "No, thanks" to these directors and stayed true to herself. That was when doors started opening.

"Whenever someone tells me I can't do something, it makes me want to do that thing ten times more, and I usually succeed," she said. "Even silly things like a former coworker telling me I wouldn't be able to get abs, so I got abs in two weeks, or a friend telling me I shouldn't try baking, so I started a cooking blog that's been well-received. I definitely attribute some of my success to this stubborn attitude."

When she started booking modeling gigs, while still holding down her full-time job, it became clear she was going to have to choose which path she wanted to pursue.

"It was really time-consuming to juggle everything at the same time," Jarry said. "I was so burned-out at my job, and at the same time I was cast in a music video that went on to have 300 million views. So, it just seemed like why not try to make this full time?"

Her family initially doubted the decision, telling her it was risky to give up a perfectly good job with health insurance and benefits to pursue a dream that might not be attainable. But Jarry knew she was ready for the next step—she just had to take it.

Despite the fact that she was only 5'5", far shorter than traditional models (a fact she was constantly reminded of by other models and casting directors). Despite the fact that few Asian models make it into high fashion or ever star in leading roles. Despite her own limiting beliefs that would pop up from time to time.

"I think I was worried at the very beginning," she said. "I was scared because if it didn't work out, how was I going to deal with an emergency? And with health insurance? I just had anxiety over that uncertainty. But it also pushed me to work a lot harder, because if I'm not working, if I'm not hustling, I'm not eating."

Her risk paid off. Within a year, she was modeling for brands like Maybelline, Lancôme, Bobbi Brown Cosmetics, and L'Oréal Paris. She leaned into her unique qualities, understanding the value in highlighting the things that made her different from everyone else, like her height, her blonde hair, her cultural background, and her experience in editorial. Directors began to take notice.

"I think because everyone looks the same it helped me to be different," Jarry said. "There are very few Asian models in the industry. What I learned was to focus on standing out, rather than on trying to fit in."

By emphasizing the things that make her special and tuning everything else out, she's been able to land multiple high-profile gigs. In addition to modeling for print, she's also appeared as herself in commercials for AT&T and Dr. Brandt Skincare, on the Netflix docuseries *Dating Around*, and as an actor in commercials for many brands.

The next step was to build up her social media presence. As a social media influencer with 800k followers and counting, she's landed campaigns with major brands like Clinique and Giorgio Armani Beauty, among others.

Suffice to say, she's earning far more than she ever did working in publishing and has more free time to be creative and pursue new endeavors. Lately, she's been pulled to start producing and recording music, something she never would've had the time to dabble in if she still had an office job. She's even been able to do some work for BuzzFeed again, this time in front of the camera.

"One of my friends says that to play it safe is actually riskier than taking any risk," Jarry said. "I think there's a lot of truth in that. A lot of my colleagues from that job have since been laid off, so it wasn't really secure. It's not like any job is really safe and certain. I love being my own boss and have never felt happier or more fulfilled. Now many of those earlier naysayers have told me my career path has been inspiring."

BIO: Jarry Lee is an agency-signed model, actress, musician, and social media influencer with over 800k followers across her platforms. Based in Manhattan, but originally from Wales and England, she is an alum of NYU and Choate Rosemary Hall. Before pivoting to a career in entertainment, Jarry previously worked for four years as a deputy editor at BuzzFeed, covering books and culture. She appeared as herself on the Netflix show *Dating Around* (season 1), as the lead actress in season 3 of *The Fever*, and in commercials for AT&T, Dr. Brandt Skincare, and various L'Oréal brands. *Authority Magazine* named her one of their

"Inspirational Women in Hollywood" in 2020, and *StarCentral Magazine* called her a "rising star to watch in 2020." She has been featured in *Vogue Italia*, POPSUGAR, Mic, Elite Daily, *NY Daily News*, *AM New York*, the *New York Times*, *Cliché* magazine, TMS, *MOVER* magazine, *Mess Magazine*, *Naluda Magazine*, and other publications.

72 AND STILL TEARING UP THE BMX TRACKS
KITTIE WESTON-KNAUER

"When they tell you that you can't, you just keep right on keeping on."

Kittie Weston-Knauer never set out to become the oldest female bicycle motocross racer in the United States, a woman who's still tearing up the tracks at age 72. She just rarely turns down a dare.

"I grew up with five brothers and one sister, and they used to dare me to do all kinds of crazy things," Kittie said. "And I mastered them all, every time."

So, when her oldest son, Max, challenged her to try BMX herself (after too many races where she yelled out from the sidelines all the things he was doing wrong), she did.

"On Mother's Day of 1988, wearing Max's helmet and his gloves, I was put upon his bike," she said. "I had never participated, and I didn't know diddly about BMX, but when your kid throws a dare at you, what do you do?"

Bicycle motocross (BMX) is a type of off-road bicycle racing. It typically involves a starting gate and then a track that includes flat stretches, small hills, and making agile turns, at speed. Racing on the track that Mother's Day in '88 gave Kittie a whole new appreciation for the sport, but her love of bikes had started long before that.

As a child growing up in the segregated South, Kittie, known affectionately by most as "Miss Kittie," was given a bike at age 10. It opened up the whole world to her.

"My father always said, 'Kittie, there's nothing that you can't do, regardless of what's going on around you,'" she said. "That shiny new bicycle opened up a whole new world for me because then I could explore a whole new neighborhood. But we understood living in the South that there were places we didn't go as African Americans and as women."

Raised by two educators, school and education were always the priority in her childhood home. In between church and school, Kittie rode around and explored her hometown of Durham, North Carolina. These rides instilled in her a sense of confidence and adventure. She'd continue to explore her city by bike into adulthood as she too became an educator and started a family in Des Moines, Iowa.

"We were a cycling family before we ever knew anything about BMX," Kittie said. "Cycling was a family activity. And then later, as an educator, I would start bike clubs and take my students through the city streets by bike. I wanted kids who were coming from all walks of life to know about the city of Des Moines, and to know about where people live, how people live, and that they could explore their city on the bike."

After that first Mother's Day race in 1988, Kittie raced again. And again. She started with local BMX races but soon began to move up to national races. In 1990, she was one of only two female BMX racers competing on the national level.

"Here I am out there with these guys, and some of them didn't like it a whole lot," she said. "There were some guys who just couldn't get by me and they complained about women racing with the men. This went on for several years at the national level."

It led to changes made by the racing organization. Today,

women have their own cruiser classes in BMX races, divided by age range. At 72, Kittie is the oldest woman out there on the tracks according to CNN and the *New York Times*, and she loves it.

"When I started racing, other women would say, 'Why are you doing that?' Kittie said. "Now the same women are coming to me and saying, 'You sure look like you're having fun,' and I say, 'Well honey, get you a bike and get out here!' We've gone from two women in the sport to thousands who are endeavoring to be a part of this. It is critical that as women we understand we don't have to put our lives on hold while we raise our families. This is a family sport."

Her work in education and her role in BMX has led to other opportunities as well. Kittie is active in her community and serves on several community boards. She volunteers at the Children and Family Urban Movement, a nonprofit that supports the potential of children, youth, and families through education, healthy living, and community involvement. She's also helped build a BMX track in her city, funded entirely through donations and sponsorships.

Though she has now retired from her work as an educator and school principal, she still routinely works with youth. She runs a summer bicycle camp and is part of a collective that helps provide bikes to her community, at no cost. She sees the racing track as her extended classroom, one that continues to teach and inspire her.

"The day you stop learning, you are dead, plain and simple," Kittie said. "Every time you get out on that track, you learn something. In life, you must continue to learn. I may be 72. I've had both hips and knees replaced because of arthritis, but every time I get on that track, I learn something new."

That's not to say it's been easy. Kittie has sustained injuries on the track. She's met men in the sport who didn't approve of her participation. She's encountered racism. But she inspires those she comes in contact with through the simple fact that she keeps getting up and getting out there, long after others have quit. And when people try to tell "Miss Kittie" that she should stop racing because it's too dangerous or she's too old, she just smiles.

"What I do is not about me, it's about all of us," she said. "That's something I learned growing up in a huge family. When you do something, you do it the very best that you can, and you never let anyone tell you that you can't. And when they tell you that you can't, you just keep right on keeping on."

BIO: Kittie Weston-Knauer, or "Miss Kittie," as she is affectionately known in the cycling world, was instrumental in the rebirth of the sport of bicycle motocross in Iowa. From 1999–2001 she rallied the Des Moines metro community, including city and county officials, on the merits of the sport of BMX for youth and adults. Since 2001, riders from throughout the United States and Canada have raced at 80/35 BMX Track located in Ewing Park on the South Side of Des Moines. Throughout the years 2001-2011, Kittie held the positions of track director, track president, and Iowa State BMX Commissioner. She was also on the National Bicycle League (NBL) Board of Directors 2010-2011. At 72, Ms. Kittie is the oldest female BMX racer in the United States.

In February 2011, Weston-Knauer was named as one of The Grio's 100 History Makers in the Making. This was in recognition as one of 100 African-Americans in the United States who are continually making a difference in their community.

Weston-Knauer is a graduate of Drake University with a BS in Education (1970) and an MS in Secondary School Administration (1973). She and her deceased husband (August 2, 2019) are the parents of two adult sons, a granddaughter, and two grandsons.

TOOLS TO TRIUMPH

The Trailblazers in this chapter were all chosen for their ability to reinvent and define their own paths. They pursued what they wanted with fervor, despite anyone who tried to stand in their way. When they came up against obstacles, they found creative solutions. When they met people who tried to dim their light, they used this negativity to burn even brighter. Here are some specific ways they got through the most difficult times.

1. **They refused to believe there were limits**

    Seriously, who says you have to live your life any kind of way? When Sandra Hart launched a YouTube channel at age 79, she couldn't have known that would lead to a staggering three million views (and counting), but she continued on, and kept putting herself out there. Because why not? She loves being in front of the camera, so she did exactly that.

    What do you love to do? Are you holding yourself back from doing those things because you worry about what others might think? What if you created, just for the sake of creation? What if it didn't matter if anyone ever saw your work? Start from a place of passion, and the puzzle pieces start to fit.

2. **They prioritized their needs**

    It took a health scare for Mirna Valerio to begin prioritizing herself and her needs, after so many years of caring for everyone else around her.

    Are you listening to your own needs? Are you showing up for yourself like you'd show up for others? How could you put yourself first today?

3. **They rewrote the rules**

    When Luciana Faulhaber was continually typecast into supporting roles like "drug dealer's girlfriend," she thought, *This stinks*! So instead of fighting with directors to give her better roles, she decided to write the script herself. By thinking of a creative way around the "rules," she was able to advance her career in spite of an industry unwilling to change.

    You can't always change the institution, but you can change your approach. How could you get creative in order to overcome a challenge you're facing right now?

4. **They knew not everyone would love them, and that's okay**

    When Jarry Lee started in the notoriously cutthroat world of modeling and acting, she frequently had casting directors telling her to change this or change that about her appearance. But she knew from the beginning that not everyone would cast her, and that was okay.

Staying true to who you are is the best way to differentiate yourself from others, no matter what profession you're in. Don't give in to the temptation to change to fit others' expectations. Give them a "Thanks, but no," and keep it moving. What if instead of changing, you enhanced that feature to further define yourself?

5. **They tuned out the negative noise**

Kittie Weston-Knauer has heard it all. Now, she just smiles when others try to tell her that BMX is too dangerous for a woman of her age.

The long and short of it? Just do you. Keep your gaze laser-focused on accomplishing what you want, and ignore the rest. People will always have opinions on how you live your life—but the only opinion that matters is your own. Are you living your life for you?

The ADVENTURERS

Running Faster Toward Your Fear

THE ADVENTURERS WHO OVERCAME "YOU CAN'T GO THERE"

"She stood in the storm and when the wind did not blow her way, she adjusted her sails."

—*Elizabeth Edwards*

Much like Miss Kittie, I've never been able to turn down a good dare. That's how I found myself wearing a harness while standing on a ledge outside of the 61st floor of the Macau Tower, preparing to jump.

"Yeesh, how crazy would that be?" I had said to Molly, trip leader and lifelong friend, just a few days earlier, when the topic of bungee jumping came up on our press trip. "I triple doggy dare you to do it," Molly said. I knew what was coming next.

Macau is famous for three things: casinos, a unique blend of Chinese and Portuguese heritage, and being the location of the world's tallest bungee jump. I had been invited to Macau along with other members of the travel media to cover the opening of a new property. I almost choked on a dumpling when Molly told me the tourism board had also booked me for an upcoming jump. I'm pretty sure I started sweating from places you aren't supposed to sweat from, like my eyelids, but I tried to keep a brave face on for the group.

After all, this opportunity was a gift. An *expensive* gift. The AJ Hackett Bungy at Macau Tower was in the Guinness Book of World Records as the highest commercial bungee jump. That kind of fame doesn't come cheap—a jump from this height costs roughly $500 with photos and video.

That night I spent hours watching YouTube videos of people doing the jump. It only made me more nervous. My hotel room was on the 23rd floor and had floor-to-ceiling windows. Standing in the window and looking down was dizzying. How was I supposed to get myself to jump from a distance three times as high?

Before I knew it, it was the day of the jump, and I was standing on that ledge outside the Macau Tower with a harness wrapped around my waist. I was nearly in tears, telling the men hooking me up to cables that I didn't think I could do it. They didn't seem to hear me.

"You'll be fine," one attendant said to me, waving me off. "I hope."

Jerk. They just kept doing what they needed to do for my safety, checking clips, hooking things to my ankles. Before I knew it, they were walking me to the edge. I felt wind surging up from beneath me, the cold sucking the breath from my chest.

"Look up," they said. One of them grabbed my head and turned it slightly to the right. "Say cheese to the camera!" I smiled a forced, terrified smile. My heart was thumping so loudly because I knew this was the moment: you say, "Cheese," and then you fall.

There are times in life, and certainly in travel, when you have to just give in. This was one of them. Up there, I had two choices: frantically knock over a couple of men while ripping the harness from my waist, making a huge, embarrassing scene in the process—or jump.

"Please push me," I begged the man standing behind me. "I can't do it, please push me."

"Okay," he whispered in my ear.

And then I fell, face first, 61 stories down.

I fell for 764 feet in 60 terrifying seconds where I didn't seem to breathe at all. When my ankle cable finally caught and I rebounded back up, I made it nearly back to the 61st floor where I had started, and had to fall straight down all over again.

Eventually this cycle stopped, and I was left dangling upside down. I took a big, *living* breath and reached in between my feet to pull a tiny pin that propelled me to a seated position. Once I was sitting up, looking out at Macau below me, I realized I was screaming. Not in fear — in elation.

When I got down, Molly was standing there, shaking.

"That was the most terrifying thing I have ever seen, and I never want you to do that again," she said.

"That's funny," I said. "Because I totally would."

When you've got a spirit for adventure, you find yourself setting the stakes higher and higher. The brave ladies in this chapter can all relate. And just as I have, they've all been told these same things:

> *You can't go there, it's too dangerous.*
> *You can't afford to travel for that long.*
> *Can't you just drop this travel obsession and get a real job?*

Following your passions, particularly as they relate to traveling the world, can trigger fear in other people. But that didn't stop these badass wanderers and it shouldn't stop you. These are the Adventurers.

THE FIRST WOMAN TO CROSS-COUNTRY SKI ANTARCTICA SOLO
FELICITY ASTON

"If it doesn't scare me, then perhaps I shouldn't be wasting my time."

Felicity Aston is a British explorer who has been traversing the Earth's polar regions for over 20 years. In 2012, she made history when she became the first and only woman ever to cross-country ski Antarctica, coast to coast, completely alone. The journey earned her a place in the Guinness Book of World Records and a Queen's Polar Medal for services in Antarctica. But prior to the undertaking, she met with a handful of experts who didn't believe she'd make it.

"When you put yourself forward, you will have a lot of people saying you can't or shouldn't do something," Felicity said. "For me personally, these are things that I can't *not* do. They've been in my head for so long that I know I'd regret it. I don't have a choice. I have to go and do it. It scared me, it woke me up with sweaty palms, thinking about not coming back, and yet I knew it was something I had to do."

At the time, other explorers seemed only interested in doing journeys to the north or south poles. As she discussed her upcoming Antarctica trip with experts around her, many questioned why she wanted to do such a thing. It didn't seem to occur to anyone that maybe she wanted to do the journey for her own reasons and out of her own curiosity.

"I had a good handful of well-qualified people who were in a position to give opinions that I really should have listened to, and they gave me very good reasons as to why I shouldn't even bother," she said. "These ranged from me not having the mental toughness, to me not having the right experience, even down to someone saying, 'But what's the point? Why should you bother if no one is interested?'"

Tackling risky journeys was nothing new for this explorer. In 2006, she led the first all-female British expedition team across the Greenland ice sheet, and in 2009, she led a group of novice skiers across Antarctic ice to the South Pole. But she'd never done any of these things alone, not tied to anyone, no one nearby to call for help if things went wrong.

As the small plane dropped her down on the ice, her bags heavy with food and supplies, she looked around at the vast white landscape and felt a ping of terror. She was alone now, really alone; the only living thing for hundreds of miles. Over the course of the next 59 days and through 1,084 miles of icy terrain, she would confront a deep feeling of isolation and fear, again and again. But for now, she simply dropped to her knees and cried.

"Instead of pretending the fear wasn't there, I had to allow myself a certain amount of time to absorb that, recognize that I was terrified, and find a way to move forward," she said. "I don't think I ever conquered the fear. The whole time I was frightened, it was finding a way to move on regardless, and some days that meant having a good cry, or using logic or reason to make myself find a more secure way forward."

Felicity was well-prepared for this journey. She had spent years working on the Antarctic peninsula at a British research base, and many months in the run up to the trip studying maps and consulting with experts. She knew which glaciers she was going to ski up, and which areas had giant crevices to avoid. She knew how to camp in the ice and snow.

But putting one foot in front of the other, day after day, required every ounce of physical and mental energy that she had. To keep her brain active and to prevent hallucinations from the extreme temperatures and solitude, she'd sing or speak to herself. To keep her spirits up, she thought of the finish line, reminding herself why she was doing this in the first place. She loved Antarctica and felt a deep association with the place. She was strong, she was prepared, and she knew that she could do it, even if other people doubted that she could.

"It's quite personal to be told that you don't have the toughness or that you're not the right type of person," Felicity said. "You try to be as thick-skinned as possible, but it's still quite hard to hear it. I ended up bundling up quite a lot of that toward the end and using it as motivation."

In all her explorations, Felicity confronts some degree of fear or risk. When we spoke about how to overcome fear, she said part of it comes down to acknowledging it.

"Let the fear in," she said. "If I'm waiting for something to feel right, it's never going to feel right. It's always going to feel scary. And it should be scary. Perhaps what I should be searching for is what feels scary."

It takes a lifetime of practice and training to be able to look your fears in the face and name them. Having now done a handful of scary things, like crossing both poles and the Greenland ice sheet, Felicity said she never stopped feeling afraid—and that's a good thing.

"Each expedition has to scare me a little bit, otherwise I'd find myself a little bit bored," Felicity said. "If it doesn't scare me, then perhaps I shouldn't be wasting my time."

Choosing to do the very thing that scares you isn't just a personal act of bravery. You never know who you might inspire in the aftermath.

"What really still amazes me is I still get emails from women—and men—who, because they've heard of one of my expeditions, have done something they wouldn't do otherwise," she said. "I find that so humbling."

BIO: Felicity Aston is the first and only woman in the world to ski across Antarctica alone. The 1,744 km, 59-day journey, completed in January 2012, also made her the first person in the world to traverse the continent purely by muscle power, without the aid of kites or machines, earning her a place in the Guinness Book of World Records. In 2015, she was awarded the Queen's Polar Medal for services in Antarctica and was appointed MBE for services to Polar Exploration. Felicity has also been elected Fellow of the Royal Geographical Society (with IBG) in London and is a Fellow of The Explorers Club in New York.

Most recently, Felicity created and led the Women's Euro-Arabian North Pole Expedition, bringing together women from Saudi Arabia, Qatar, Kuwait, Oman, Sweden, Slovenia, Russia, France, and the UK, who together reached the top of the world by ski in April 2018. She has written three books, including *Call of the White: Taking the World to the South Pole*; *Alone in Antarctica* (with a foreword by Joanne Lumley), and *Chasing Winter: A journey to the Pole of Cold*. Find out more about her at felicityaston.com.

TYPE-1 DIABETES WON'T KEEP HER FROM TRAVELING THE WORLD
CAZZY MAGENNIS

"I have an ambition to be the first female type 1 diabetic to go to every country in the world. And once I do, I'm gonna say, 'There you go, you said I couldn't go to certain places, but I've been to them all.'"

Cazzy Magennis was diagnosed with type 1 diabetes at age 16, and right then and there, she was told that her dreams of traveling the world were over. But Cazzy wasn't about to accept that.

"I wanted to see the world," she said. "But my doctors all told me 'No, you can't, you need to stay in one place and you should think of a more stable career.'"

All she ever really wanted to do was travel. Growing up in Northern Ireland, she craved a lifestyle that would take her around the world and introduce her to different cultures. So, at age 18, she decided to start traveling solo.

But she also had to consider access to insulin. In order to travel safely, she'd have to travel with insulin and have a backup plan to make sure that she could find it anywhere she went. Insulin has to be kept at a certain temperature, and if you're traveling for long periods of time in between refrigeration, your insulin could go bad. As a diabetic, if she didn't get enough insulin, she could end up in the hospital and the situation could become fatal.

It took some getting used to, but Cazzy said that for the most part, traveling as a diabetic has been easier than she expected. Except for a week she spent on a boat in the Amazon, when her insulin got hot, with no refrigeration in sight. To prevent her blood sugars from getting too low in the heat, she had to rely on food and fruit juices.

"It was not a great situation, but I got through it," Cazzy said.

There was also a time in Norway when it was so cold in her campervan that she had to sleep with her insulin wrapped in socks next to her body to keep it from freezing.

"Before I go, I always prepare for the worst-case scenario," Cazzy said. "I've had my insulin frozen in a hotel. A full month's worth of insulin that froze and died, but rather than freaking out, I was making a plan of where I could get insulin from there. It's all about planning for things to go wrong and having a backup plan."

When she travels, Cazzy tries to stay in a place where her insulin can stay cool in a fridge, and where she can have some control over what she eats. This often means staying in rented apartments, with access to full kitchens, rather than staying in hotels.

"Since I started traveling, my health and diabetes control has been the best it's ever been," she said. "I feel so much more confident because I've experienced so much. It's tiring at times, and it takes work, but you *can* travel the world with type 1 diabetes."

In 2016, after quite a few successful trips, Cazzy and her boyfriend Bradley decided to start a travel blog where she could put all of the information and resources she was gathering in one place.

Her blog, *Dream Big, Travel Far*, shares travel tips, as well as information for diabetic travelers. She also has created a community of diabetics who travel. As a traveler, Cazzy continues to raise the bar for herself. So far, she's been to over 60 countries and counting.

"Honestly, the fact that they said I couldn't do it is what made me have to figure out how to do it," Cazzy said. "I have an ambition to be the first female type 1 diabetic to go to every country in the world. And once I do, I'm gonna say, 'There you go, you said I couldn't go to certain places, but I've been to them all.'"

BIO: Cazzy Magennis is a type 1 diabetic from Ireland with a zest for life and ambitions to travel to every country in the world. She's been traveling full time for almost five years now and has no plans to stop. Cazzy believes we are all capable of anything and wants to inspire others with chronic conditions to know that it's possible to achieve your goals, whether they be traveling or otherwise. You can follow her on her journey around the world at Dream Big, Travel Far.

LIVING HER WILDEST
DREAMS, IN ITALY
ASHLEY BARTNER

....

"I kept thinking, 'Why not? Why not us? Why can't we live our wildest dreams?'"

When Ashley Bartner and her husband started telling people that they wanted to move from their Brooklyn apartment to Italy, everyone thought they were crazy.

"What are you running away from?" her grandmother-in-law asked them.

It wasn't that their lives were bad, per se. They were both working professionals with good jobs, her husband an executive chef, and Ashley in guest relations. It's just that they wanted something more.

After a small wedding, they traveled to Italy. It didn't take long to fall in love with the country: the food, the wine, the atmosphere. They loved the pace of life they found in romantic, small towns. Everyone they met seemed to be really living their lives, not just working all day.

"What if we lived here?" Ashley asked her husband, a few days into the trip. They spent that afternoon dreaming of it, but then returned home and fell right back into the minutiae of everyday life.

Still, the idea wouldn't leave her. While mindlessly scrolling real estate websites one night looking at options in other cities, she found her mind drifting back to Italy, again and again.

"This is cheesy, but it was also Oprah's 'Live your wildest dreams' season," Ashley said. "I kept thinking, 'Why not? Why not us? Why can't we live our wildest dreams?'"

So one day she opened her computer and Googled, "Buy a home in Italy." When her husband came home that night, she met him at the door.

"I said, 'Oprah says you should live your wildest dreams and I think we should move to Italy,'" she recalled. "He just looked at me and said, 'Okay, first of all, don't start a conversation with 'Oprah said.' And second of all, if we're going to do it, let's do it all the way. I don't want to half-ass this. I don't want to be a couple that people ask ten years later, 'Wait, weren't you guys going to move to Italy?'"

So they sat down and started creating a blueprint for how to actually make it happen. They drew upon her husband's background as a chef and let themselves dream. What if they could live in a property that also functioned as an inn for guests, and her husband could offer cooking classes? They started writing up a business plan.

With a pretty clear vision, the newlyweds started telling everyone they knew about their upcoming move to Italy. Most people initially assumed they wanted money from them and were reluctant to take this idea seriously. But money wasn't their main concern.

"I knew we couldn't wait until we had the money to plan this," Ashley said. "I knew we had to just figure it out, and then we'd find the money."

After a few trips to Italy, they settled on a little-known region called Le Marche, near to Umbria in the central region. They had found an investor in New York who was willing to help them buy a property, but the deal fell through at the very last minute.

"I remember that evening my husband said to me, 'What do we do, we just lost ten-thousand dollars,'" she recalled. "And I just said, 'We go forward.'"

When things are meant for you, they find you. Though their initial property didn't work out, Ashley had been working with an Italian tax accountant who believed enough in their vision to help them when no one else would. He suggested renting a house, an option they hadn't even considered before when they were so focused on buying.

In pure Italian fashion, he also happened to know of a rental that might be available—*if* the owner liked them enough. The two went anxiously to the meeting, introducing themselves and sharing their plans. After a few hours of conversation and some hearty laughs, the owner of the house agreed to the deal. He said he recognized a bit of himself in Ashley's husband, and the deal was secured over a handshake and a glass of prosecco.

Three months later, with Italian visas in hand, they moved to Italy and into the home. It took another two-and-a-half years for them to fix up the 500-year-old farmhouse, perfect their business, get to know the culture and to work on cooking classes. The journey has been full of twists and turns, but before they knew it, the inn was full almost every night.

"You have to just have an unwavering belief that you can do it," Ashley said. "Having a partner you're doing something like this with can be helpful, because if one person starts to doubt the vision, the other is there to support."

These days, in addition to running a busy inn, cooking classes, offering market tours, and hosting private weddings on the farm, the couple also help other people follow their dreams of moving to Italy via private virtual workshops. Their journey continues to be full of unexpected surprises.

"When we told people, at 25 years old, that we wanted to move to Italy, they thought we were crazy," Ashley said. "But it was to our benefit that we were young when we moved here, because the locals kept thinking, 'Where is your mother? These orphans have moved to Italy and we have to take them in!' And they taught us how to live like Italians, and be a neighbor, and how to be a part of a community, and we didn't realize that was something we were seeking as well. To find people who have become like family to us is one of the most fulfilling parts of this journey."

BIO: Ashley Bartner wears many hats: expat entrepreneur, host-extraordinaire, free-range chicken wrangler, consultant, food and travel writer/photographer, and filmmaker. Ashley is the founder and owner of La Tavola Marche (farm, inn, and cooking school) established in 2007. She has contributed to numerous international magazines, including more than five years writing a monthly column in *Italia!* and *Taste Italia!* She strives to promote sustainable and culinary tourism.

THE WOMAN WHO TRAVELED TO EVERY COUNTRY IN THE WORLD
JESSICA NABONGO

"When you figure out who you are, and you accept yourself wholeheartedly despite all of your flaws, despite what people have told you your entire life, when you just decide, 'I am enough,' that will make so many people really uncomfortable."

When Jessica Nabongo made history in 2019 by becoming the first Black woman on record to travel to every country in the world, most of her friends, family, and community celebrated right along with her. But not everyone was as supportive.

"A lot of people didn't think I would do it," Jessica said. "But the concept of not finishing never crossed my mind. I knew I could figure anything out, and I did."

Born into a Ugandan immigrant family, Jessica's life of international travel began at the age of four. She knew the world was open to her, and her parents encouraged her to see it.

By the age of 21, she was earning nearly six figures in a pharmaceutical sales job and had purchased her first home, yet she wasn't fulfilled. Jessica knew she wanted more. She could no longer deny the desire she had to go out and see the world.

Despite the uncertainties at the height of the economic recession in 2008, she quit her job, moved to Japan to teach English and began blogging. A year later, she launched a travel blog called *The Catch Me If You Can.*

"By 2009, I had already had the desire to visit every country in the world," she said. "I would always say I would visit every country before I was 40, it was something I just said. It was something that I wrote about on my blog, and I just knew it was something I wanted to do."

After years of working for other people while traveling around the world, Jessica decided it was time to work completely for herself. Her freedom was more important to her than anything else.

"Everything I do in my life is to allow me to experience freedom," she said. "It's for the freedom of my time, meaning I only do things I want to do, period. Freedom of location, on any given day, I can be anywhere I want to be and with my laptop and camera, I can be making money from anywhere. That is really what drives me now. I think the different interactions I've had with people around the world make me think about life and success differently."

In 2017, Cassie de Pecol was inducted into the Guinness Book of World Records as the fastest person to travel to every country in the world. Reading about de Pecol's journey led Jessica down an Internet rabbit hole where she discovered a community of country-counters. Her goal had always been to see every country in the world by age 40, but now, she decided to try to complete her mission by age 35, and to be the first Black woman to do it. In sharing this goal more publicly, she started gaining traction in the press, too. But with the good, also came the bad.

Toward the end of her journey, another woman was claiming that *she* was actually the first Black woman to travel to every country, but she couldn't provide proof. Online, people were vicious. Some tried to discredit Jessica's quest and said really hurtful things. As she got closer to the finish line and toward completing her goal, some of her closest friendships were also tested.

"As you change, the people around you may have to change," Jessica said. "For me, that's the biggest thing I learned and how I have got to a place where I'm comfortable. Over my life, society has told me that because I have dark skin, I'm 'ugly,' I have short hair so I'm 'not feminine.' I could do things to adjust myself to the outside world, but there's still going to be critics. You just have to build up that armor."

In October 2019, on her late father's birthday, Jessica officially completed her goal and became documented as the first Black woman to travel to every country in the world. More than just arranging visas and handling travel logistics, Jessica attributes this accomplishment to her community who encouraged her to the finish line.

"You have to step into your greatness, for the good of the whole," she said. "People along the way were just so kind to me and so generous, and once I realized that [my journey] was so much bigger than me, that was the fuel that took me to the finish line. I couldn't quit because this wasn't my journey anymore, it was *our* journey. Eventually, I was able to say we did it. I was the vessel for the journey, but we did it as a community."

But the side of success that no one really ever talks about is the fact that not everyone you love will be able to grow with you and your accomplishments—and that's okay.

"It may make people who are super close to you turn on you, and you won't know why, and it's because your confidence is brushing up on their insecurities, and there's nothing you can do about that." Jessica said. "Getting to the place of wholeheartedly accepting yourself is such a journey. But you can't go back on that path for anybody."

BIO: A Detroit-born Ugandan-American, Jessica Nabongo got her start with traveling when she was just four years old, and now the former United Nations employee has become the first Black woman to travel to every country in the world.

She is a cultural ambassador, travel writer, photographer, and entrepreneur whose work is about changing the travel narrative and making the travel space more inclusive. She is the founder and CEO of Jet Black, a boutique luxury travel firm that specializes in tourism to countries in Africa, the Caribbean, and Central and South America; as well as The Catch, a lifestyle brand featuring goods acquired during her global adventures.

Jessica is committed to raising cultural awareness and encourages people to think positively about other countries and the world at large so that we don't miss out on opportunities to have amazing experiences with our neighbors.

As an advocate against the use of single-use plastics, Jessica has used her platform to raise awareness of this global issue. She reminds us that even though it may not seem like it is an issue in our neighborhood, city, or state, it is a huge issue globally and as we are all part of the same ecosystem, we all have a responsibility to be more conscious of how we use plastic.

As an influencer, Jessica's travels and expertise have been captured by national outlets such as *Forbes,* The Huffington Post, Fox 2 Detroit, *Conde Nast Traveler*, BBC News World Service, the *New York Times*, CBS News, and more. In March 2019, she was named one of the 30 Most Powerful Women in Travel by *Conde Nast Traveler.*

SHE CYCLED FROM
LONDON TO ISTANBUL
LAUREN PEARS

"I thought if he could do it, I could do it too."

Lauren Pears wanted to ride her bike from London to Istanbul, but everyone around her told her it was too dangerous a journey for the then 23-year-old to undertake.

"A lot of people thought I was crazy," Lauren said. "I didn't have cycling experience, and there wasn't really much of a reason as to why I chose to do it. I watched a documentary about a guy who cycled around the world and I thought if he could do it, I could do it too."

At the time, Lauren felt trapped by her environment. She was working in marketing, and felt that she was becoming someone she didn't want to be. She had no long-distance cycling experience and limited solo travel experience, but getting on her bike gave her a feeling of freedom, and having a goal as ambitious as cycling to Istanbul carried her through the stresses of her day-to-day life. As with most good ideas, Lauren kept returning to one simple question: why not?

"I planned this for a year. I thought about it, I trained for it, I went to the gym a few times a week," she said. "But you really can't train for cycling seven hours a day other than to just do it."

So, she did. In 2019, Lauren set off via a ferry from London and began her ride through France. Her route would take her through France, Switzerland, Germany, Austria, Slovakia, Hungary, Croatia, Serbia, Bulgaria, Greece, and Turkey. To save money and to have the most flexibility, she camped along the route each night.

"The initial ups and downs of feeling alone have long gone and have been replaced by a content solitude," Lauren wrote on her blog, *The Planet Edit*, 28 days into her ride. "Some days, I feel a liberating sense of freedom—everything I need is packed onto my bike and I can just accept and enjoy wherever the road takes me. I have no one to compromise for, no one to dictate rest stops or what we should have for dinner."

Throughout her 89-day ride, she met a few other people who were also doing long-distance rides, mostly men. Though they congratulated one another for their respective journeys, some of them kept telling Lauren how dangerous it was for her, a woman, to do the same—despite the fact she was already doing it.

One night, she was camping next to a guy named Matt who was cycling to Iran. A couple came over to them and everyone got to talking about their journeys. When they heard about Matt's ride they said, "Wow, amazing!" When Lauren said she was riding to Istanbul they said, "What? On your own? Won't that be dangerous for a young girl like you?" These little comments started to really bother her.

"All my friends were fairly supportive, but when I was on the road, people I didn't even know would be like, 'Why are you doing this, you're a small, young woman, it's not safe,'" Lauren said. "That part would annoy me because they'd never say that to male cyclists."

Apart from a few drivers who slowed down to whistle at her, Lauren said she had hardly any negative experiences throughout those 89 days. In fact, her trip introduced her to exactly the opposite: a beautiful world, full of friendly and hospitable people, who went out of their way to help her when she needed it.

In Serbia, the locals ran outside and greeted her with fruits and water. In Turkey, a kind man gifted her watermelon and tomatoes. In Germany and Austria, as she rode through the colorful Wachau Valley, Lauren marveled at the scenery: an abbey, perched high on a hilltop surrounded by vineyards and a flowing river below.

She finally felt like she was actually *living* her life, instead of just going through the motions, dreaming of what she'd do "one day." When she got to Serbia, she met two cyclists from Thailand who were also riding to Istanbul. They joined forces, cheering one another on in those final days through Turkey.

"A lot of times when the going got really tough, it was such hard work," Lauren said. "It was hot weather, dangerous roads, I got carpal tunnel syndrome halfway through. It was a very physically tiring thing. When I finally got to my hostel in Istanbul, that was such a good feeling."

Reaching and accomplishing her goal has given her a sense of accomplishment that still lingers—despite all the people who told her it was silly or impossible or unsafe along the way. The risks of course, were always there, but the rewards were so worth it.

"If you want to do something like this, you just have to go for it," she said. "There's always going to be worries. It sounds like a massive feat, but like anything, you just have to take it one day at a time."

BIO: Lauren Pears is a travel writer and blogger from London. With a passion for backpacking and outdoor travel, she aims to inspire people to get off the beaten path, explore the great outdoors and travel more sustainably. Follow her blog at theplanetedit.com.

TOOLS TO TRIUMPH

Traveling is one of the best ways I know of to connect to your own sense of personal strength and power. But getting on that initial plane can be terrifying. It takes a lot of courage to push your suitcase right out of your comfort zone and into another country. Whether moving abroad or just exploring for a few weeks, traveling takes planning, financial risk, and a fair amount of logistics. Add to that fears voiced by well-meaning friends and family, and travel becomes something that many *never* find the time, money, or space to do. These brave Adventurers all decided to ignore the blockmakers and travel the world anyway. Here's how they got through things when life as an adventurer got rough.

1. **They let the fear in**

    Felicity Aston encountered fear just about every day that she was cross-country skiing her way through Antarctica. Fear is one of our most basic human instincts, but too often, we try to suppress it or ignore it—causing it to pop up or manifest in other parts of our lives. It sucks to be afraid, so we spend years running from fear. But what if instead of running, we let the fear in? That's what Aston did on the ice.

    Ask your fear, *What are you trying to teach me?* Look around and see if you're really in any danger. For children who grew up in environments where they were frequently afraid, this is especially important. If you take nothing else from this book, please consider your relationship to your own fear and evaluate it often. Where does it come from? When do you feel it? How does it hold you back in life? What if instead, you could imagine it as an old friend, and let it in?

2. **They prepared for the worst**

    As a type-1 diabetic, Cazzy Magennis must do a lot of planning before any trip. This means she has to get on the phone and call different hospitals, hotels and medical clinics to find out where she might be able to find insulin should she need it. In preparing for the worst-case scenario, she is able to release a bit of that anxiety and enjoy each moment of traveling.

    Can you do the same? Think of a dream you have. Then, write out every single worst-case scenario you can think of. Get them all out of your head, so that you can free up space for excitement to take over.

3. **They gave themselves permission to dream**

    When Ashley Bartner started dreaming about living the life of her wildest imaginations, she realized it didn't seem that far from impossible. She was fortunate to have a partner who shared those dreams and ambitions, and who was willing to take the leap with her. When Ashley realized she felt the pull to live in Italy, the rest became about taking a series of steps to make that happen. One of the biggest things that helped is that she and her partner started telling everyone about their plan, which kept them accountable to it.

What are your biggest dreams? What small steps can you take toward enacting them? Who can you confide in to keep you accountable?

4. **They developed a practice of self-love**

As Jessica Nabongo explains, when you set a big goal for yourself and you actually *do* it, it can make people uncomfortable. Your accomplishments will brush up against their insecurities. In her case, she also had to face scrutiny from anonymous Internet trolls who said hurtful things. To get through this, she developed a practice of unshakable self-love and acceptance. Instead of listening to the noise encircling her and letting it devastate her, she went further inward. She prioritized herself and her mental health.

Love yourself harder, above anything and anyone else.

5. **They trained, to an extent, and then they just went for it**

Lauren Pears didn't have any long-distance cycling experience before she decided to ride her bike from London to Istanbul. She just knew she wanted to do it. So, she spent some extra time at the gym. She planned her route and shopped for camping supplies. And then the time came to just go for it.

You can't ever be *fully* prepared for anything and there will always be surprises (how could Lauren know she'd get carpal tunnel from riding on rocky roads?) Don't get stuck for too long in the preparation phase or it will turn into procrastination. Give yourself a deadline and a consequence. Buy the non-refundable ticket. Invest in the bike. Prepare, and then go for it.

The VISIONARIES

Building Resolve to Never Doubt Your Vision

THE VISIONARIES WHO OVERCAME
"IT CAN'T BE DONE"

*"Failure will never overtake me if my determination
to succeed is strong enough."*

—*Og Mandino*

Have you ever felt the urge to do something that makes no logical sense? In March of 2008, I was in my final semester at the University of Arizona when I woke up with an unmistakable desire to move to New Zealand.

I really can't tell you why New Zealand. I didn't know anyone there, I had never been there, I had never even really met anyone who had been there. And yet, I thought about it constantly.

Everywhere I looked I saw signs for it: commercials all seemed to suddenly be featuring New Zealand's landscape, billboards I passed by every day now had kiwis on them. At the time, I was freshly out of two back-to-back internships at the biggest newspapers in the state of Arizona and I worked as the news editor of our university campus paper. Regional papers in Iowa and Montana had called with job offers. I turned them down, certain my next step involved travel.

My professors questioned my decision to take extended time off to travel, and what it might do to my career. "Think about it," they said. "You can't ever replace that lost time, and what about the gap in your resume?"

I didn't care. As a graduation present, my family kindly gifted me a trip to Fiji, New Zealand, and Australia, and a friend and I set off for six incredible weeks of adventure. When we finally reached New Zealand, I knew I was home.

Being in the Land of the Long White Cloud (as it's called) made me feel like I was my best self. Driving along the North Island's jagged coastline felt like taking a B-12 shot.

Many years later, I would sit with an astrologist who would overlay a map of the stars at my birth with a map of the world. Lines and lines of energy crisscrossed right through New Zealand. Being in New Zealand, he said, was for me the astrological equivalent of standing beneath a spotlight—and I could feel it.

When I returned home from that trip, I was more determined than ever to live there. I made a list of actionable steps: I applied for a working holiday visa, which allows American travelers under the age of 30 to work in New Zealand for one year (Australia also has this option).

I manifested every night, imagining myself there with perfect clarity. I was so certain of the decision that I sold my car before I ever received news that my visa had been approved. Then, I sold every single thing I had, down to my pillows and bedding.

It still didn't amount to much. I arrived in New Zealand with $400 in my pocket, a backpack, and a visa good for one year.

Little did I know, that year in New Zealand would change absolutely everything in my life. It was my introduction to the feeling of abundance, and of what a life of infinite adventure could look like. I found a community of backpackers who taught me to view the world as a playground.

We worked to *live*, not the other way around. Money helped us to see more and *do* more. It was the opposite of how I was raised. The scarcity mindset and the fear of "lack" that I was accustomed to was just gone. No one there ever told me that I *couldn't*, or that any place was beyond my reach.

The way I viewed my own potential changed, as I recognized that nothing in life is ever set in stone. If I decided I wanted to stop working in journalism and become an accountant, for example, nothing said I *couldn't* (it was just that I'd have to work for it). The very Earth itself seemed smaller—in the span of just one day, I could be on the complete other side of it, if I chose to be. Everything seemed possible.

Even my work was playful—after a brief stint as a housekeeper in Dunedin, I got a job with a company that ran *Lord of the Rings* tours out of Queenstown. Guests would frequently arrive for their tours fully clad in robes and capes, speaking Elvish. Because why not?

I moved into a two-bedroom house that had six people living in it, and those people became (and still are) my travel family. I didn't yet know I'd end up writing about travel professionally, or that those roommates would end up being lifelong travel companions I'd see the world with. I didn't yet know that I'd fall head over heels for a skydiver who lived in the north of the country and have my heart royally broken when my visa ran out.

I didn't yet know that I'd tap into what felt like a river of possibility, an entirely different way to live life; that I'd end up starting multiple businesses that helped other women access this same river, too. But all of that happened, after I said *yes* to a persistent and nagging voice telling me to move to New Zealand where I knew absolutely no one, with only $400 to my name.

The brave women in this chapter have all felt the same calling in their lives. Though people around them told them that they "can't do that" or that they were "crazy" or that their dreams were "illogical"—they refused to listen.

You don't always have to know *why* you're being called to do something—your only obligation is to walk down the road of doing it. What could your life become if you followed through on that nagging idea that won't leave you?

When you're open to receiving messages, they come from everywhere—and often, in your dreams. Many of the ladies in this chapter started businesses from dreams or ideas that came to them in the middle of the night.

From launching Emmy Award-winning television shows to creating a product with many millions in sales, these ladies *actualized* their visions and quite literally made their dreams come true. These are the Visionaries.

DANCING HER WAY ACROSS THE WORLD
MICKELA MALLOZZI

"This little voice was just saying, 'Don't listen to everyone, you have to make this happen.'"

In the middle of a cold January night in 2010, Mickela Mallozzi woke up with a vision.

"It was like this projection was coming out of my eyeballs," Mickela said. "I could see full dances and full costumes and carnival, I could picture my crew, I could picture everything."

She grabbed a notebook and started writing furiously, waking up her husband who was sleeping next to her. Mickela had been taking dance classes since she was three years old. She also loved to travel. What if she could combine her passions and create a television show where she traveled the world and learned the local dances of each country? The idea set her soul on fire.

But she was a dance instructor with zero experience or connections within the television industry. So, she started asking friends of friends for introductions to producers.

"Hands down, never going to happen," Mickela recalled. "That's what they'd tell me. Every single one of them said the same thing over and over, that it was a decent idea, but that I'd never be the host of it, and that they'd have to hire an actress to be the host of the show."

Dejected, Mickela kept thinking: *if I'm selling the show but have nothing to do with it, then what's the point?*

"In April, I decided that I was just going to do it myself," she said.

The child of immigrant Italian parents, Mickela still had family in southern Italy. So, she hired three friends to operate cameras and sound and they all flew to Italy, staying in her grandmother's farmhouse. It was a dream come true. Plates of Nonna's homemade pasta were passed around the table by night. Days were spent exploring the region, dancing, and getting comfortable with the camera.

Mickela put together a sizzle reel and pitched it to production companies, with a goal of getting it on the Travel Channel. But after signing an exclusive one-year contract with a production company, news broke that the Travel Channel had just picked up an identical show.

"That was my first heartbreak," Mickela said. "To hear that someone was already doing the show I want to do. And she was much prettier, and had a TV background, *and* was on the network I wanted to be on."

With the Travel Channel out, her production company decided they wouldn't be pitching it to anyone else. But they also wouldn't give Mickela her footage back, unless she paid them $30k or waited the full year for their contract to run out.

"That was my second heartbreak, and in that moment I

could've just given up," she said. "But I didn't want the project to end, and this little voice was just saying, *don't listen to everyone, you have to make this happen.*"

She couldn't quit. So, she decided to take her idea online, creating a blog and producing online videos. She gave up on all her old footage, at least for the time being, and started fresh on YouTube. But she still really wanted it to be on TV.

One day, Mickela found out about a PBS conference that was happening nearby. She snuck into the conference, where she met a programmer from the local public television station who loved her idea. They asked her to produce 13 episodes by the next month. It was happening! Except Mickela didn't have 13 episodes of a show, she had 5-minute YouTube videos.

"I don't believe in 'fake it till you make it' but I do believe in saying yes and figuring out the details later," Mickela said.

From that point forward, Mickela threw herself into the project and never looked back. She stitched a season together with the footage she had and started joining travel conferences, finding travel meetups in New York City, immersing herself in the NYC travel industry.

Everyone from her former life looked at her like she was crazy for quitting her job to chase this dream in the middle of a recession, but she didn't care. Mickela knew she had to make this happen—and she did.

Her 13-series show, *Bare Feet with Mickela Mallozzi*, aired on NYC Life, a local public media station, where it grew in popularity and eventually expanded to national distribution on public television through PBS. Today it is broadcast nationally to over 106 million homes.

She's won four Emmy Awards, including two for best host. In her most recent acceptance speech for best host, she dedicated it to every producer who told her she'd never be on television, because they gave her the drive and determination to prove them wrong.

"People came up to me after and said it was the best F-U speech they'd ever heard," Mickela said.

The show has expanded to three seasons and is available on Amazon Prime to every English-speaking country in the world. It is distributed in Hong Kong and in parts of Russia and Greece, and on in-flight programming on international airlines and cruise ships.

But for Mickela, the best part is the personal connections she's made.

"I started this completely selfishly," she said. "I wanted to travel the world and dance and learn every single dance I can along the way. And then I realized, there are so many levels of the story. People feel connected to me as their friend, and we're giving them a different view of a place they might have thought was scary, and we're breaking that myth. We're all similar. We all need food, shelter, love, and a little bit of dance and music to be happy in life."

Despite the producers and well-meaning family and friends who told Mickela that her idea was impossible, her show continues to expand into new outlets.

"I was the black sheep outcast turned local hero," she said. "For me it's a privilege to be able to say: I had this idea, which everyone thought was fucking nuts, and I had to work for it for ten years before people actually took me seriously."

BIO: Mickela Mallozzi is the four-time Emmy Award–winning Host and Executive Producer of *Bare Feet with Mickela Mallozzi*, a travel series highlighting the diversity of dance which airs on PBS stations nationwide and is available on Amazon Prime Video globally. A professional dancer and trained musician, Mickela decided to start a journey around the world, taking her camera with her to follow dance in the lives of everyday people wherever she went. From rediscovering her family's heritage in Southern Italy to dancing tango in Buenos Aires, the series covers Mickela's adventures as she experiences the world, one dance at a time. She has been featured in the *New York Times, O, The Oprah Magazine, Forbes, AFAR, Travel Channel, Dance Magazine*, and more, and she has performed on various television shows including *Sesame Street* and *The Doctor Oz Show*. For more information on Mickela and her dance adventures, go to TravelBareFeet.com

SHE LAUNCHED HER OWN LITERARY JOURNAL AND BROKE BOUNDARIES
AMY GIGI ALEXANDER

"Well, perhaps these difficult things happened to me, but I am not defined by them. Instead, I am defined by what I choose."

No one gave Amy Gigi Alexander permission to launch her literary travel journal, *Panorama: The Journal of Intelligent Travel.* In fact, just the opposite.

"Not everyone supported it, and some told me I was out of line to try to make it or change an established genre," Amy said. "Most of the people in powerful editorial roles in travel, both commercial and literary, were older white men, and me showing up saying I wanted to make something that challenged that power of gender and color was uncomfortable for them."

Panorama is a literary journal that aims to publish the world, from Lagos to Timbuktu, and put the spotlight on voices of color who are often excluded from other publications. In creating something entirely new, Amy was shifting power, and some people didn't like that. She was told by some in the literary world that she "couldn't" do this, and that she had to "put in her time" before she could take on revolutionizing a genre, she said.

"I had stepped out of line," Amy said. "I did receive quite a lot of hate mail, mostly from white, privileged writers. White editors in power stopped answering my emails and ignored me completely. I was told the project would fail and that if I did not have the support of certain people, it would not work."

Yet, Amy was perhaps the perfect person to launch *Panorama*. As a self-taught writer who struggled through school with a learning disorder, she had come up against "gatekeepers" her entire life. As a young girl, she dreamed of being a writer, but her learning disabilities made this dream feel elusive. At home, she experienced sexual abuse, but in the wake of this sorrow, she found her inner fire.

"As a young girl, I was molested by a close relative repeatedly and I think at some point, during that time of incredible sorrow and isolation, and even disbelief that it happened, I decided to make myself into someone," Amy said. "There was a lot of loneliness in those early years and I did not have the tools, moving into adulthood, to even have dreams yet, let alone make them happen. But there was a glimmer in me, something that did not die off, and that bit of shine got brighter as I aged."

Writing was one of her outlets, and at an early age, Amy began a daily writing practice in a journal. Years later, when a friend admitted that she had found her journal and had read it cover to cover, she told Amy that she was a good writer and encouraged her to think about it as a career. After years of traveling and working as a nanny, Amy decided to explore her potential as a writer. She began by attending a travel writing conference.

"The conference was intimidating, and I wanted to leave every hour, but I forced myself to stay although the dynamics of being at a literary event made me want to disappear into the upholstery of my seat," she said. "I ended up winning the contest they had, and my career began."

In 2015, she began submitting pieces to different publications, all the while suffering from imposter syndrome. Expecting rejection letters, she instead found praise. Opportunities continued to come her way from here. The only problem, Amy said, is that the journals publishing her work hardly had any diversity to them. That frustration became the impetus to creating her own publication.

TELL HER SHE CAN'T

"There really were few literary journals focused on travel," Amy said. "Not every story is commercially viable in the travel category. Why not make a place where [those stories] could go, that had status and a high bar?"

In the end, any initial resistance to *Panorama* she received became a blessing. It forced Amy not to rely on others or follow existing models, and instead gave her a clean slate to reimagine what a literary journal *could* look like.

Launched in 2016, *Panorama* immediately made its mark not just in travel writing but as a model for diversity from the top down; its mission unmatched, and its works taught in travel writing courses at universities. In 2020, the journal and Amy were mentioned in the much-esteemed *Routledge Travel Writing* introduction as movers and shakers in the genre.

"I am naturally attracted to what is hard to do," Amy said. "I enjoy the push of moving outside the lines, and it gives a real sense of fulfillment to say, 'Well, perhaps these difficult things happened to me, but I am not defined by them. Instead, I am defined by what I choose.' I am an example of a self-made powerful woman, using that power for good."

BIO: Amy Gigi Alexander is a writer, editor, publisher, and explorer. Her literary journal, *Panorama: The Journal of Intelligent Travel*, publishes four issues a year and also publishes books. Her work has been published in more than a dozen anthologies, as well as commercial outlets and journals. She has taught travel literature in such places as the American Library in Paris, the Louvre, Banff Mountaineering Festival, AWP, and Santa Fe Workshops. Her book, *Twenty-one Journeys to Elsewhere* is out in 2021. She lives in San Miguel de Allende with many cats and dogs.

PLAYING MUSIC ON A
CARPENTER'S HANDSAW
NATALIA "SAW LADY" PARUZ

"Because I had no people to ask questions of, I figured out my own technique that was very different from others' technique, and it was good because it enabled me to push it forward and be different from everyone else."

Photo Credit: Rod Goodman

Natalia "Saw Lady" Paruz always wanted to be a dancer, having trained in dance for many years. But one day, when she was 20 years old, she was hit by a car while crossing the street from Lincoln Center in New York City.

"That put an end to my dance career," she said. "My whole childhood, I thought this was what I wanted to do, this was my dream. Now I was faced with trying to figure out what I wanted to do with my life."

It was a tough adjustment. Seeing her struggle, her parents took Natalia on a trip to Austria to get her mind off things. They went to see a tourist show, where one of the performers was playing music on a handsaw. Natalia was instantly enamored.

"It was the first time since the accident that I actually felt excited about something," she said. "I thought, *Wow, this is so cool,* and there was this fire that started to grow inside of me. I wanted to learn how to do this."

So, she did something that she'd never done before and hasn't done since: she went backstage after the show. She found the musician and begged him to teach her how to play. He said no. She offered him money, he still said no.

"He said, 'Go home and pick up a saw,'" she recalled. "Imitate what you remember seeing me do on stage and figure it out."

Disappointed but determined, Natalia went home and

borrowed a saw from a friend's tool shed. She tried to play music on it, but she could only get six notes to come out. The saw was older and rusty. She wondered what a newer saw would sound like.

"I went to the local hardware store and I was trying out all the saws there and the owner was furious about the sound I was making and kept saying, 'Who is whistling!'" she said. "He looked at me like I was from Mars when he saw what I was doing, because who tries saws this way?"

The new saw opened up a variety of new sounds and octaves, and Natalia began practicing. Her mother, a classically trained pianist, was supportive of this new venture, but told her that to be a musician, she had to take lessons. Except there was no one around to give lessons.

One day, a musical agent came by her house to meet with her mother. Natalia asked if she could play the saw for him, and her mother agreed. He loved it! He then asked if Natalia could play the saw during one of her mother's next performances. That was all the assurance her mother needed.

"After that, my mother was like, 'Okay, I guess there is something here, it's real,'" Natalia said. "So, that really helped the whole situation with my family."

Her friends were supportive, but questioned her often, asking, "What is this? Why do you want to do this? Is there a call for this? Is this something there's a need for?"

She kept practicing regardless, falling more in love with playing the musical saw, noticing that the way the instrument moved reminded her of dancing. While working a job at a Broadway theater selling souvenirs, she'd sneak off into the adjacent parking lot to practice during showtime.

"I would sit in the most remote corner of that parking lot because I didn't want to be seen or heard," Natalia said. "Playing, it was just for me."

But one day, while practicing, a father and his son started watching her in the parking lot. After a song, he handed her a $5 bill. At first, she didn't understand—but then she realized she just earned her first tip for a performance. She ran into the theater and told her coworkers what had happened.

During that period on Broadway, many nearby shows had long intermissions and hundreds of people would come outside to smoke. So her coworkers convinced her to go out front of the theater and play for them.

"My friends dragged me out and they placed an empty box in front of me and one of them put a one-dollar bill inside and they said, 'Play.'" Natalia said. "I started to play and people started to gather around me and they were clapping their hands together and smiling, and they started to put money in the box."

At the end of that 10-minute intermission, she had more money in the box than she would've made in her entire shift in the theaters. That did wonders for her confidence. Soon, she was practicing on the street, instead of in the corners of parking lots. As her confidence grew, she began playing on larger and larger streets and in the New York City subway.

Opportunities began presenting themselves, as they often do when you're on the right path in life. Her neighbors, after hearing her play through the walls, passed her information onto the local Salvation Army. They invited her to come and play, and then passed her information onto other chapters. Natalia also began developing an audience in the NYC subway. The response to her music was almost unanimously positive. Almost.

"When you play on the street in NYC it's like a perpetual audition whether you realize it or not," she said. "In the subways, of course, not everybody likes every kind of music and there were people who would walk by and say, 'I hate this music,' but then right after that, I'd have someone say, 'Oh, this is so cool.' I just learned to not pay attention to people in the subway who put me down."

Playing in the subways led to other opportunities as well. Today you can hear Natalia's saw playing on movie soundtracks such as HBO's *The Jinx*. She is also in the Guinness World Records for having organized the "Largest Musical Saw Ensemble," a group of 53 saw musicians, who played as part of the NYC Musical Saw Festival she initiated and ran for 11 years. She has performed in Carnegie Hall, Madison Square Garden, and Lincoln Center.

"I thought dance was the thing for me, but then something had other plans for me, whether you call it providence, or faith, or a higher power, and it was like, 'No, this is not what you're meant to do, *that's* what you're meant to do.'"

And the man who refused to give her lessons so many years ago? Natalia has nothing but gratitude for him. The time-honored tradition of the art form mandates that you should be self-taught. If you pick up a saw and can't figure it out on your own, then don't bother, it isn't for you. However, if you pick it up and can make it play on your own, then this is your path forward.

"I'm very grateful to him for refusing me, because by doing that, he enabled me to experience the art form in the old-time, traditional way. He forced me to try it out by myself," she said. "Because I had no people to ask questions of, I figured out my own technique that was very different from others' technique, and it was good because it enabled me to push it forward and be different from everyone else."

BIO: Natalia "Saw Lady" Paruz has spent more than two decades bringing the rare art form of playing music on a carpenter's saw to audiences around the world. Her playing can be heard on movie soundtracks such as HBO's *The Jinx*, *Time Out of Mind* with Richard Gere, Fox Searchlight's *Another Earth*, *Dummy* with Adrien Brody, and others. Natalia has played the musical saw with the Israel Philharmonic Orchestra conducted by Zubin Mehta; at the Spoleto Festival in the orchestra of "Monkey—Journey to the West;" with the Westchester Philharmonic Orchestra; the Royal Air Moroccan Symphony Orchestra; the Riverside Orchestra; the Amor Artis Orchestra; the Manhattan Chamber Orchestra; and at Lincoln Center's Avery Fisher Hall with PDQ Bach composer Peter Schickele; and with the Little Orchestra Society. November 2007 marked her Carnegie Hall debut as a musical saw soloist and

June 2008 marked Saw Lady's Madison Square Garden debut. She was chosen by *Time Out New York*, the *Village Voice*, the *New York Press*, and the *New York Resident* for their "Best of New York" lists.

HER CAREER PIVOT IS HELPING THE WORLD MANIFEST ITS WISHES
ALEXA FISCHER

"You can't change your childhood, you can't change your family, but you can change yourself."

Alexa Fischer was playing dead on the set of the television show *Bones* when she was suddenly overcome with a sense of dread. As she lay there on the dirty floor of the Los Angeles Times building, fake blood coming out of her nose, she couldn't shake the sense that she had deviated terribly from her true path in life.

"I'm lying there, fifteen hours into the shoot, and I have a total meltdown in my mind," Alexa said. "I thought to myself, *Oh my god, what have I done with my life?* I have spent so much energy working toward this thing that I imagined that I wanted, I was methodical about it, I treated it like a business, and on the outside, it looks like I'm successful at it, but I'm dying inside. I feel like I'm wasting my life. This is not what I came here to do."

The thought came as a shock. Was this really how she felt? She had spent years in acting school, investing so much in formal training, working her way up to this point. She had suffered through hundreds of auditioning indignities to make it all the way onto the sets of prestigious shows and movies. What right did she have to feel this way? Worse still, if she really didn't want to act, what *did* she want to do?

"At that moment, I asked for a sign," Alexa said. "Okay, universe, you've got to give me something because this is not working."

Two days later, she got a call from a friend she had met while filming a commercial. That friend was starting a new business and she needed a media coach for a new client. Without thinking, Alexa said yes.

She began by creating a video course that would help people learn to express themselves by exploring the mind, voice, and body—condensing years of her own acting experience and training to help others break free from fear. Ten years after she made that initial course, she had over a dozen courses and over 115k students around the world.

Between coaching, teaching, and motherhood, her life was quite full—but then one day, she had a crazy idea in the shower.

"Boom, a thought came to me," she said. "I heard the name 'Wishbeads' and I saw intention-setting jewelry where you could write your wish and wear it tucked inside your jewelry, so you would have a visible reminder of what you want to create in your life."

That idea would go on to become her next entrepreneurial venture. Though she didn't have any experience in manufacturing or jewelry design, she did know the power of manifestation—she had turned her desires into real-world outcomes over and over throughout her years as an actress.

"Life, for whatever reason, wants to convince you that you can't get what you deeply desire," Alexa said. "When I was an actress, I found it so frustrating that so many random people stood between me and my dream jobs. It didn't matter how talented or prepared you were. That bothered me, so I said, 'I'm going to green light myself.' I'm going to challenge myself to create my own thing. That way I can take responsibility for my own success."

She knew that Wishbeads was so much more than just inspirational jewelry. Alexa wanted to create a movement. She wanted to help others realize and harness their own internal power.

To get started, she launched a Kickstarter to help fund the project. In 30 days, it became fully funded at $25k and surpassed its goal. As it so often goes when you're walking your true path, she connected organically with a woman on Twitter who would become a trusted adviser helping her secure her amazing manufacturing partner.

"Early in my acting career, I knew you had to fake it 'till you make it," Alexa said. "But when you're building something on your own, learning how to ask for guidance is everything. I've learned so much as a business owner, and it's always evolving."

Since its inception in 2016, Wishbeads has helped thousands of people around the world to manifest their deepest desires. Her company has been featured on *The View*, *Good Morning America*, and the OWN Network. She has hit epic sales goals, built a team, and helped thousands of people. Her really big wish is to have one million people wishing at once—an event to help people tap into their best and brightest lives.

"You can't change your childhood, you can't change your family, but you can change yourself," she said. "Wishbeads aren't magic. *You* are magic! You can decide to take action and create the life you deserve to live."

BIO: *Wishbeads* founder Alexa Fischer is an actress, teacher, author, and motivational speaker whose work helps people go after their dreams, build their confidence, and break free from fear. Using online courses, private coaching, and her goal-setting jewelry line, Alexa's work has reached tens of thousands of people. She has shared her techniques with future leaders at the Girls Athletic Leadership School and current leaders at companies like Trader Joe's, SONY, Google, PepsiCo, and IBM. She's been featured in *Fast Company*, *Forbes Women*, numerous podcasts, and in an appearance on *The Today Show*. Her Wishbeads jewelry is carried in boutiques around the country and has been worn by celebrities, friends, and folks young and old.

You can see her in action at alexafischer.com and her creations at Wishbeads.com.

instagram.com/wishbeads.official

youtube.com/user/alexafischer

SHE BUILT AN
EMPIRE FROM A DREAM
SANDY STEIN

"If I die tomorrow, you can write on my tombstone, 'She did everything she ever wanted to do.'"

Sandy Stein had been working as a flight attendant for 30 years when one night, she had a dream that her father (deceased) told her to invent a product. She woke up and sketched out the idea furiously.

It was the start of what would become Finders Key Purse: a hook that could attach to your purse, so that your keys wouldn't fall to the bottom of your bag. A cute decal sat on the outside of the hook, making it both fashionable and functional. It could also be used to attach a panic alarm or pepper spray, so that if you really needed it, you could get to it quickly and easily.

The dream felt like a gift and excited Sandy, but she had no idea how to actualize it. She did, however, know someone who did: her husband, who worked in the gift industry. She excitedly told him about the idea and waited for him to share in her enthusiasm.

"He said, 'That's nice, but you can't do that,'" Sandy recalled. "He said, 'You're a flight attendant, all you know how to do is serve food. You didn't go to college; you have no qualifications for this.'"

His words stung, but Sandy didn't want to let her idea go. She knew deep down that this idea could really be something, even when her husband recruited three of his friends to echo his skepticism, calling her product a "cute little idea." One of his friends, however, did show a little interest. He offered to buy the idea from her outright for $50k.

"As soon as he said that, I thought, *if it's worth it to him, then it's worth it to me,*" she said.

It was a sign that she was on the right track. Sandy decided right then and there that no matter what, she was going to bring this product into existence. So, she started networking in the manufacturing and production industry, spending late nights researching as much as she could about creating a product.

When it came time to launch her prototype, she knew exactly who she'd turn to for help selling it: her network of flight attendants, who she'd been flying with for decades.

"In December 2004, we launched with twenty friends," Sandy said. "But they started telling their friends, and by the end of 2005, I had over two thousand people selling the product."

By the end of that first year, they had sold over one million units. With a thriving business, Sandy began expanding her product catalog by creating different decals. Suddenly, the businessmen who had rejected and tried to minimize her idea were knocking on her door.

"I made a name for myself because everyone thought, 'Here she is, 53, a flight attendant, who didn't have a clue what she was doing,'" Sandy said. "And look at what she did."

Finders Key Purse has since sold over 12 million units and reached many millions in sales. Through the highs and lows of the business, Sandy was able to learn and thrive in an industry she had known nothing about previously, and retire from her work as a flight attendant. Her product created so much affiliate income for her sales team of flight attendants that it helped them to pay their mortgages. It allowed for philanthropic charity work, which Sandy was able to do in underserved communities. And it continues to create income for Sandy and three employees today.

"I believe that I was a vessel for this product," Sandy said. "I am very tenacious and I rarely quit, even when it gets so hard that I think it's impossible. This little product brought so much good into the world and into my personal situation with my family."

Sandy and her husband divorced not long after her initial dream, before her product grew to its full success. The wild, exciting, entrepreneurial ride she's been on ever since has been largely hers to enjoy.

"There are always people who doubt your capabilities," she said. "Stay true to your dreams and block everything else out. When I was starting this business at 53, I was told that I was too old. If you can't when you're old, and you can't when you're young, when can you? If I die tomorrow, you can write on my tombstone, 'She did everything she ever wanted to do.'"

BIO: Sandy Stein quit college to become a stewardess, but planned on returning to college after a fun year of flying. Thirty-five years later she retired from Delta Air Lines with a degree in life skills, and an 11-year-old son. During her career as a flight attendant, she always sold something to supplement her income, so it was no surprise to her friends when she invented a product to sell. Finders Key Purse was born the year before she retired, and thanks to her flight attendant team (women telling women), Finders Key Purse made it onto the shelves of thousands of retail stores. It's been 16 years of the wildest roller coaster ride you can imagine, and Sandy is proud to say that she is still finding new homes for her patented Finders Key Purse.

TOOLS TO TRIUMPH

How many times have you had a great idea for a business... and then promptly let it fade? Me too. Life just gets in the way sometimes, unless you take swift action, like the Visionaries mentioned in this chapter. Chosen for their ability to act on inspiration and create something tangible from potential, these Visionaries stayed in service of their dream when the rest of the world tried to tell them it couldn't be done (or that it couldn't be done by them). Here's what they did to stay focused.

1. **They got creative when they encountered obstacles**

   When Mickela Mallozzi signed a deal with a production company that was pitching her idea to the Travel Channel, she was elated. When that fell through, she could have easily quit right there. Sometimes the universe tests us, challenging us to either keep fighting, or walk away. If she had quit, she may never have become the four-time Emmy Award–winning host of her own TV series, which has aired nationally on PBS and internationally through Amazon Prime.

   Don't quit when the going gets tough. How can you get creative instead?

2. **They didn't let other people limit them**

   When Amy Gigi Alexander wanted to begin her own literary journal, the response from her community was generally positive. However, there were certainly people who told her that she had to "put in her time" before doing such a thing or that this was "not the way it was done."

   Who says? Naysayers only have the power we give them. Challenge the gatekeepers and follow the jetstream created by your own idea. Has anyone ever tried to limit you in this way before? What would you say to them now?

3. **They manifested and asked for signs**

   Alexa Fischer kept getting messages from the universe telling her she was not on the right life path, but she didn't know what that right path was just yet. It wasn't until an idea came to her in the shower that everything clicked. You can't force inspiration, but you can call it toward you by continuing to ask the universe for signs and finding quiet.

   Consider keeping a notebook by your bed and in the bathroom—the places where inspiration seems to visit most frequently!

4. **They built their confidence slowly**

When Natalia "Saw Lady" Paruz wanted to play music on a carpenter's handsaw, people thought she was nuts. She didn't have instructors to turn to. She didn't have a band to practice with. She had to teach herself and slowly practice, which she did at home and in the corners of New York City parking lots on her work breaks. Eventually, she gained the confidence to play near Broadway. Years later, she'd end up in the Guinness World Records. Practice, practice, practice, and keep going.

Have you ever felt the pull to do something that no one else really understood? Something other people maybe thought was "out there" but that you loved so much that you didn't really care? That's the energy you want to tap into and use for future projects!

5. **They removed the blockmakers from their lives**

When Sandy Stein approached her husband about her business idea, his initial reaction was to mock her. Rather than support her vision, he listed all the ways in which she wasn't the right person to create this business. Over time, she stopped surrounding herself with people who tried to pull her down (including her husband, who she divorced).

It isn't always easy to distance yourself from a loved one who doesn't lift you up, but you must. Either establish boundaries and areas of conversation you will and won't entertain, or remove or limit their interactions with you and your life. It is imperative that you surround yourself with people who lift you up. Don't let the blockmakers derail you.

The PREVAILERS

Surviving Literally Anything

THE PREVAILERS WHO OVERCAME
"YOU CAN'T MAKE IT"

*"I can be changed by what happens to me. But I
refuse to be reduced by it."*

—*Maya Angelou*

*You need a job? Here, work for me. Need a place to live? Move
on in! Need a plane ticket? I'll fly you out here. Need some food?
Here you go!*

Growing up feeling like I had to beg for love left me in the
same repetitive cycle when it came to my adult relationships: I'd
do anything—offer everything—to retain the affections of men
who were never right for me. I would give, give, and give some
more. In return, I'd find myself in situations where my partners
stole from me, tormented me, and gaslit me. They were unfaithful
and unapologetic about it.

This left me in a cycle of emotional debt and perpetual sacrifice (and so much *drama*) that lasted the span of almost a decade. What I didn't realize then is that constantly offering help to others is one of many ways in which I was punishing myself. I was self-flagellating to get recognition, so that someone would finally *see* me and say, "Oh wow, she's so good, look at all she does." And then maybe I would be.

Before I did the work on myself necessary to end this cycle and remove *all* of this *pressure* that I had been unknowingly putting on my romantic partners, I spent years trapped in these loops, caught in relationships that were full of hurt, confusion and pain.

It finally came to an end when I devoted a solid year to focusing exclusively on myself. I stopped pretending I was fine and sought help. I threw everything I had at healing—I did hypnotherapy, Reiki, and cord cutting. I saw a therapist consistently. I saw an astrologer and a medium. I practiced forgiveness. At times, it felt endless, until one morning I realized I had come out the other side.

I was lying in bed with my current partner—my big, sweet love—when I started being flooded with memories of all my past hurts. So many abandonments, cruel words, heartless decisions, playing scene-by-scene before me in rapid succession. I couldn't escape it, so I just started weeping, for the little girl within me who once pronounced her name *Koggy*, who spent so long waiting for someone to show up for her. For the girl who could never seem to understand she hadn't done anything to warrant her suffering. For the woman who had been trapped in the same pattern of behavior for decades without even realizing it.

I'm sure this was all very confusing to my boyfriend, lying with me casually on a Sunday as tears streamed down my face onto his stomach. But he held me just the same, reassuring me that I was safe, until I finally floated out of my body and realized that I was. With, or without him.

Safe. Worthy. Infinite.

The women in this chapter are all Prevailers, those who have overcome some deep and painful traumas, many involving their closest relationships. Healing is a winding journey, not a destination—we are forever works in progress.

At times, these ladies doubted themselves because of the hundreds of times they were laughed at, mocked, or told they "couldn't make it" by the people closest to them. Despite it all, they found the power to rise up, the strength to leave, and the courage to develop their own identity, voice, and talents. Whether overcoming painful breakups, recovering from harrowing childhoods, or fleeing conservative religions, these women have flourished, post-trauma. These are the Prevailers.

SHE REFUSED TO BELIEVE SHE WASN'T STRONG ENOUGH
AMANDA MATTHEWS

"I kept thinking, I can get through it, there is a purpose in this that's going to make me better."

Amanda Matthews grew up a Baptist Christian, born abroad to a set of parents who were working as missionaries at the time. She loved growing up within different cultures, and so at the age of 19, she decided to become a missionary herself. She moved from her small hometown in Kansas to Brazil, feeling nothing but excited about the future. But what she couldn't have known at the time, was just how hard it would be for her to come back home.

"I moved from Kansas because I had a passion in my heart to be with people, to learn about other cultures and to interact with someone who wasn't the same as me," Amanda said. "While I was there, I met this charming man who opened his heart to me and shared my faith."

He was smart, charismatic, and strong. He was her first boyfriend, and she trusted his opinion on everything. The two fell in love and got married. They started a family, and all seemed to be divine, at first. But soon after they got married, he became more possessive and controlling.

When they opened an orphanage as part of her mission, he enrolled in the Brazilian military and started climbing the ranks.

"As he made his way up in the military, he became more and more abusive," Amanda said. "I kept on thinking, *is this a cultural thing? Is this normal? Is this just me?* It was also that I was in a foreign country, by myself. At first, I was just this adventurous girl, but being with him slowly changed who I was, because I looked up to him and I valued his opinion as a person I loved."

The abuse began in small ways. He would criticize her as she worked to learn and speak Portuguese, saying she was stupid and that she shouldn't speak because she was embarrassing him. But then things became more violent. And then that violence escalated.

"First I would deny it and say, 'Oh, he had a bad day at work,'" Amanda said. "He kept telling me, 'You can't leave me because you're not smart enough to make it on your own,' and I would believe him. He would say, 'If you leave me, you're going to go from trash can to trash can to try to find food,' and things just started escalating, but it was done in a way that was like, 'I'm saying this to protect you.'"

He started controlling her every move, placing a tracking device on her phone under the guise of "keeping her safe." Anytime she took money from an ATM he'd get a notification about it. The couple had two children by this point, a girl and a boy, and Amanda started thinking about what their life would be like as they got older.

"I stayed married for nineteen years, and I finally realized that what he did to me, he was going to do to my children," she said. "That's when I woke up. But it took me two more years to say, *I need to get out, I need to get home.*"

Getting out wouldn't be easy. She had no money, no phone, and she was ostracized from her faith for wanting a divorce. She managed to make a quick escape to the house of an acquaintance, a friend of a friend she met through her father. Her plan was to stay there while she filed for a restraining order, which should've taken three days.

Only it didn't take three days, it took 30, because the police knew her husband. By this point he was the Secretary of Defense for her state, Brasilia, and she had no proof of the abuse, even though he was actively hunting her, house-by-house.

Thirty days later she finally succeeded in getting the restraining order. He couldn't come near her, but she also couldn't go back home and get her belongings.

"I had nowhere to go, and with no job I couldn't pay rent," Amanda said. "It took ninety days for my first hourly check to come through, and we were going from house to house trying to stay out of his precinct."

Her husband had full access to tactical military equipment and tracked her down several times. She and her children moved every month to get out of his grasp. Amanda started filing paperwork with the Brazilian courts to be able to bring her children back to the United States with her, which required getting them passports—something he would also have to sign off on.

"It took me three years of legal work, and during all of that he sued me thirteen times," Amanda said. "It was so challenging. I had no idea that was going to happen. It took three years until I finally made it."

Slowly but surely, she did eventually get the kids Brazilian passports, and then American passports. As they touched down in Atlanta, Georgia, with three long years spent in hiding and in fear behind her, Amanda finally exhaled.

"I never thought of myself as strong, I just thought, *This is what I have to do, this is the only choice and so I will do it*," she said. "He did say I'd never get across the border alive, that I could keep moving around Brazil, but I'd never get across the border because he'd find me. Once I got off that plane and stepped out into Atlanta it was like, Yes, I did it. I did it just to show you."

Of course, settling into life in the United States wasn't easy either. Amanda had $250 to her name and her children had to learn English from scratch because they were never allowed to speak English in the family home. In many ways, they were starting all over again. But they were safe, and had some initial support through family. As soon as she landed, Amanda threw her phone away.

"The thing about toxic people is they do have charm, they have a side that draws you in and keeps you in," she said. "I could see that if I had fallen into this, how so many other women also fall into this, because it's gradual. It's people who you love, who you admire, who you look up to."

To reclaim her voice and her identity, which was erased from her for so many years, one of the first things Amanda did was start writing a book she titled *Shattered Sanctuary*.

Then she began a long and ongoing process of figuring out exactly who she was. She started with making small decisions.

"I'd ask myself, do I like fishing?" Amanda said. "Do I like hiking? Is it okay if I don't?"

She also began dating someone who helped her find the answers to these questions by doing more of these little activities with her. Slowly, she regained her voice.

"Now I am thankful for what I went through because it made me stronger, it made me find a voice and realize I have a lot to say," Amanda said. "Before, I was this quiet little mouse with no voice that was afraid to even voice my opinion, and now I have a voice and it's strong and I'm happy with who I discovered."

Her children, who were 13 and 15 when they left Brazil, also started blooming in their new lives, discovering their own identities more and more. Amanda started an orchid business, a flower she always loved while in Brazil.

"I keep thinking, *You told me I was going to eat out of the trash can, and here I am running a business that I love*," she said. "It reminds me of the good parts of Brazil, and believing in yourself, and believing in God. Through all the chaos, I kept thinking, *I can get through this, there is a purpose in this that's going to make me better.* I used that pain to get through it and I've learned so much about myself. I'm still learning."

BIO: While working in Brazil as a missionary, Amanda June Matthews was also a theology professor, motivational speaker, and a women's pastor. Now that she's back in the United States, she teaches about abuse and how to overcome it. She also runs an orchid store called Orchideria. Amanda spends her free time enjoying nature hikes with her children. She also loves to bike, dance, and play with her dog, Max. On weekends, they explore new campsites, canoe, and fire up a barbecue.

THRIVING, AGAINST ALL ODDS
STEPHANIE PLYMALE

"No one had high hopes for me. I had to have them for myself."

Stephanie Plymale's childhood story isn't the typical backstory you'd expect for creating a happy and successful life.

"I look at my childhood as a kidnapping, where I was taken from place to place to place," Stephanie said. "My childhood story is really a story of neglect, abuse, and trauma."

Her earliest memories find her and her five siblings in a car with their mother, who suffered from mental illness and multiple personality disorder. Stephanie regularly went hungry as she and her siblings wandered the beaches of Mendocino, or as they moved from one temporary house to another as her parents ran from the law and sought their next fix.

As her mother moved in and out of jail and psychiatric hospitals, she ended up as a ward of the State of California, passed back and forth between foster homes and her mother's care.

Stephanie says she always felt invisible. She refers to herself as a "forgotten child." Few people took kindness on her and supported her in any sort of long-term growth. Forgotten and left behind by the education system, she remained illiterate until the age of 10, when one of her mother's boyfriends taught her how to read.

It would've been really easy for her to give up on herself. But Stephanie didn't. Instead, she fought to create a life of stability, turning her trauma into power and becoming a successful mother, entrepreneur, and author.

"Everything I've ever accomplished I've done through sheer willpower," she said. "While most people have the voice of a parent encouraging them to achieve, I had to conjure my own voice. No one had high hopes for me. I had to have them for myself."

Against all odds, Stephanie graduated high school. She married her high school sweetheart at the age of 19, and credits part of the reason she was able to get through it all to him. His support held her steadfast when the world around her became chaotic. He was a guiding force that reminded her that her future was worth fighting for. They have now been married for over 35 years.

"He helped to save my life," Stephanie said. "He was really the main person who always believed in me."

In the darkest times, Stephanie would close her eyes and imagine a home full of beautiful furnishing and decor. She had little frame of reference for what to aspire to, but she knew what she *didn't* want, by observing what she lived with.

"I was always looking for what I wanted to become, looking to the people I admired," she said. "That was key for me. I had low self-esteem because of where I came from."

Stephanie went to college, and decided to study interior design, finding success within the industry. She built a successful interior design business, and then decided to take her work in the industry one step further–buying an interior design school that had been struggling.

Everyone thought she was crazy, that she'd lose all of her money, that it was a doomed endeavor.

"One of the vendors said, 'This school is a failure and a joke and so are you,'" Stephanie said. "But when you've lived the majority of your life feeling like you have nothing to lose, it creates this fearless thought process."

The school didn't flop. In fact, under her leadership, it flourished—and so did the students. She's gone on to grow the school to three locations, and her website celebrates the stories of many of the hundreds of graduates who have created successful careers.

"One of the things that propelled me was that I was so forgotten about in school, I felt like a nobody always, so I created a school where everyone is valuable," Stephanie said. "We are so invested in every single one of our students, and we have wonderful alumni who feel very supported. All of this came out of my longing for that feeling in my own life."

After years of personal development work and therapy, Stephanie also got to the place where she could write her story. She published her personal memoir, *American Daughter*. It was immediately purchased by HarperCollins and is scheduled for a full relaunch in 2021. In *American Daughter*, Stephanie tells her incredible story of intergenerational trauma, forgiveness, redemption, and healing.

"Trauma just keeps going and going and going, and you have to break the cycle," she said. "But it can be broken. One of my superpowers is that I'm resilient. I feel like I've made every mistake that you can make—once—because I learned from them all. Now when I have a dream or desire to do something, nothing stops me."

BIO: Stephanie Thornton Plymale is the owner and CEO of Heritage School of Interior Design. Heritage is headquartered in

Portland, Oregon, and also operates in Denver, Colorado, and most recently expanded to Seattle, Washington. Heritage School of Interior Design is an intensive program designed to fully equip students for a career in interior design by combining a hands-on education with a full complement of technical courses. Prior to taking over Heritage School of Interior Design, Stephanie owned an independent design firm for 18 years, serving hundreds of residential and commercial clients. Stephanie's greatest joy in owning and operating Heritage is fostering and promoting the success of its students. Over 100 students graduate from Heritage each year and many of these students have gone on to win prestigious awards and start wildly successful businesses and careers.

Stephanie is the author of *American Daughter*, her memoir, which became an instant Amazon bestseller. Stephanie is also a mother of three and has been married to her high school sweetheart for 30 years.

A NEW, EXPANSIVE LIFE AFTER RELIGION
RAE MASTER

"There's zero shame in being a strong-willed, independent, badass woman."

When Rae Master was 23 years old, she fell in love. He was handsome and charming, kind and smart. But getting to know him on a deeper level wouldn't come so easily.

"I was working in a restaurant when I met him," Rae said. "He was charismatic, charming, and everybody loved him. We started talking a little bit, and I could see potential in the relationship, but then he told me that he was one of Jehovah's Witnesses and that he couldn't date outside of his religion."

At that point in her life, Rae was craving stability. The child of a broken home, she saw something in the faith that she yearned for. Everyone in the organization seemed to have happy families and lives. His family in particular. They were warm, kind, welcoming, and fun.

"Between the prospect of the man of my dreams by my side for the rest of my life, his family and the friends I made in the Kingdom Hall, and the vast education and consistency in the organization worldwide, I felt I had nothing to lose by being baptized in the faith," she said.

But Rae realized quickly she did indeed have much to lose; from her independence, individuality, and determination, to lifelong friends and family. She was told she couldn't socialize with those outside of the organization, which meant her after-work happy hours with coworkers would have to end. She had to distance herself from her entire family, who were outside of the faith.

She was told she couldn't vote, and should remain politically neutral, which meant she had to repress her strong opinions on politics. Members also can't condone LGBTQ+ lifestyles, and they also can't strive for "the things of the world" which include career success, notoriety, awards, higher education, and money.

Jehovah's Witnesses believe we're living in the end of times, and that in this generation or the next, the world as we know it is going to change into a paradise, Rae said. For that reason, there's no need to plan for the future, or put money away for retirement.

"It's one thing if you need to put bread and butter on your table, but the second you have to work overtime, you're using time that should be spent in religious meetings or studying the Bible," Rae said. "That was hard for me too. I was living in Orange County, California, at the time and we had some affluent families in our congregation. I felt like, how did the men, as heads of households, get to be where they were without being repressed like I am? It was okay for them, but if I wanted to pursue my master's degree it was like, 'Hang on a second, that's not a worthwhile investment.'"

Yet still she didn't openly question the rules, not wanting to come off as disloyal to a faith that was so new to her. But the list of *cant's* only grew and grew. While the couple were dating, they couldn't go out together without supervision, which made really getting to know each other difficult. Of course, anything sexual was off the table, prior to marriage. Within a year of her baptism, the two were married.

"There were a lot of things we struggled through," Rae said. "I was generally happy, but I internalized my stress, which resulted in stomach problems."

They continued to follow every rule, attending meetings twice a week, Bible study with his family once a week, and knocking on doors every Saturday to "share the good news." As conflicted as she was about the fundamentals of the faith, she continued on with conviction that this was how the rest of her life would be spent.

Then, five years into their marriage, her husband came home and told her he had cheated and that he wanted to end the marriage. She was stunned. She suggested therapy, and meeting with the congregation elders, to determine how they could fix it. One other thing you're not supposed to do in the religion? Get divorced.

"He said, 'I've been dead inside the entire time we've been married,'" Rae recalled. "I will never forget those words. I was so shocked I didn't know how to process it."

She left for a work conference that week, and by the time she came home, he had moved out. Initially, Rae had planned to stay in the religion.

"But I started to realize I was getting anxiety every time I had to go to church," she said. "It was tearing me up, and that was when I realized I can't keep doing this."

The elders of the church didn't try to stop her from leaving. That's when she thought, *the trap is in my own head*. But the return to her old life wouldn't come easily. She struggled with depression, anxiety, and RTS, or Religious Trauma Syndrome, as her therapist explained. She felt nervous every time she went out with a beer for a coworker, always looking over her shoulder waiting for someone to scold her. She felt guilt three times a week when she believed she should be at meetings. She was terrified of dating because of the strict guidelines she abided by for years. She felt ashamed to wear tank tops or skirts above knee length. Finally, at the age of 31, she found herself trying to figure out how to plan for a future, alone.

"It sounds ridiculous, but it was so ingrained in me that, *you can't, you can't, you can't,* that even in coming out of the religion I still felt like I couldn't do so many things," Rae said.

Things quickly fell apart over the course of the next year. She lost her job because she "wasn't smiling enough," and she was left with an apartment and a BMW she couldn't afford to make payments on alone. She got sued in the small claims court by a fraudulent landlord as she tried to move into a new place on her own. She ended up in the hospital with kidney problems.

But little by little, things began to improve. She found another job and began to gain back some of her independence. She moved to a beautiful apartment on the beach and ran up her credit card to furnish her apartment. As she healed from the loss of a religion that required her to give up so much, she had the space to decide who she wanted to be from this point forward.

"I got rid of that fucking BMW," Rae said. "My mom had always raised me to be independent, and I just took every step erasing what wasn't me and replacing it with what was me."

Inspired by reading *The Crossroads of Should and Must* by Elle Luna, Rae decided it was time to give herself free reign to explore any and every interest she had.

"It was a phase of my life where it was like, if you want to do it, just do it, because nothing is going to stop you," Rae said. "I went through the gamut of every hobby and skill you can think of. If it crossed my mind, I did it."

She took Krav Maga classes. She traveled to Guatemala to

volunteer, building houses. She tried pottery (and hated it). She saw a therapist. She rescued two dogs. Nothing was off-limits anymore, but ultimately, she decided Orange County no longer suited the person she wanted to be. She needed a completely new start. So, in 2019, Rae left Orange County and moved to the Pacific Northwest.

She bought her own home and started her own business. She now actively invests in her future.

"Religion is so scary," she said. "I was such a smart and logical person, and it still bamboozled me. "If it can tug on your heart strings the right way or tap into your deepest needs, which for me was finding love, stability, and a family, it can take you over. But I don't regret anything about that chapter of my life. It taught me, more than anything, that while growth and evolution is healthy, it's vital to stay true to myself. And that there's zero shame in being a strong-willed, independent, badass woman."

BIO: Rae Master was born and raised in a small town on the central coast of California by her mother, to whom she credits her perseverance, sense of humor, and creativity. After high school she attended an overpriced trade school for graphic design, which enabled her to create branding and websites for a number of small businesses over the years, making entrepreneurship her creative outlet. She spent 15 years in Southern California before realizing she felt out of her element and relocated with nothing more than a full car and her two dogs to the Pacific Northwest. Now she's embracing her independence and freedom. Rae is living out her dreams of gardening, camping, cooking, and DIY-ing, all while working as a full-time creative director and selling real estate on the side. Next up? She needs a farm. With a lot of baby animals. An animal sanctuary. She dares you to tell her she can't.

THIS DOCTOR AND BLOGGER REFUSED TO LET RACISM LIMIT HER

DR. NADEEN WHITE

"I really think it's important to have some kind of foundation or somebody who believes in you, even if it's just one person, to help you fight against all that negativity that you face when you have a dream and you have so many people telling you that you can't."

When Nadeen White was 10 years old, she and her family moved to America from Jamaica. Her dream was to become a pediatrician. But almost immediately after moving to New Jersey, she started experiencing racism.

"My second day on the playground someone called me the N-word," Nadeen said. "I had never even heard that word before. Storekeepers wouldn't take money from me. Rocks were thrown at me walking home. Someone told me to 'go wash my skin.' This was New Jersey in 1981."

Though she was a great student and a fast learner, her teachers kept denying her opportunities, even refusing to believe she was doing her own homework when she landed on the National Honor Society and rose to the top of her class.

"All of my teachers gave me a hard time, they all thought my parents were doing my homework," Nadeen said. "Teachers didn't even believe I was getting these grades. No one believed I was doing my own work."

She realized quickly and with dismay that a different set of rules applied to her that didn't seem to apply to other students. She knew she'd have to work twice as hard for the same opportunities. Her parents encouraged her to keep her head down and keep putting in the work.

"My parents really believed in the American dream," Nadeen said. "They believed that if you wanted to be a doctor, you were going to be a doctor, and that you could do anything you wanted to do if you worked hard enough."

Nadeen stayed focused on school. Her first goal on her path to becoming a doctor was going to the University of Virginia. Again, her counselors told her it was going to be too difficult of a school for her to get into, despite the fact she was getting straight A's in AP and honors classes. She applied anyway and was accepted.

"Then when I got in, I was told it was because of affirmative action," she said. "I was told that I got in just because I was Black and not because I was smart. Not because I had straight A's and was tenth in my graduating class. None of that seemed to matter. I was told that I took a seat from someone else."

Those undergraduate days were very stressful. Nadeen started having panic attacks, even breaking out in hives before her pre-med classes. To get through it, she formed a supportive base within her study groups, full of other students who could understand the pressures she felt. Her family continued to support and encourage her.

"When I got into medical school after those four years, I really felt like I did it against all odds," Nadeen said. "I had to find that support and create that support, because my advisors were just not helpful, and they didn't believe that I could do it."

At the age of 25, she graduated from medical school at Rutgers University. Today, she has been a practicing pediatrician for over 20 years.

"I really think it's important to have some kind of foundation or somebody who believes in you, even if it's just one person, to help you fight against all the negativity that you face when you have a dream and you have so many people telling you that you can't," she said. "For me, I know that was based on color. Nobody could really accept the fact that I was a little Black Jamaican girl and I was going to be a doctor. Still to this day, I am proud that I persevered and did it."

She's since taken her career even further, carving out a specific and unique niche that combines her two passions: medicine and travel. In addition to working as a pediatric doctor in hospital medicine, she's also a travel blogger who has been a source for media outlets like CNN on topics related to both travel and medicine.

"When I started a travel blog, people would say, 'Why are you doing that, you're a doctor,'" Nadeen said. "And I would say, 'Are you allowed to pursue only one thing in life?' I'm now a blogger by day, and physician by night."

In developing and expanding her travel blog, *The Sophisticated Life*, she's found achievements and opportunities that she would have never otherwise found—like becoming an *O, The Oprah Magazine* brand ambassador.

"Go after whatever you want," Nadeen said. "Don't let people tell you what that is. They'll say, 'Well you have this, so you shouldn't need that.' Don't listen. Go after whatever you want."

BIO: Dr. Nadeen White is a "travel blogger by day, physician by night." She has over 20 years of experience practicing medicine and over six years of experience as a travel content creator. Her award-winning travel blog The Sophisticated Life covers affordable luxury travel, food, and wine as well as health and medical topics related to travel. Nadeen is also an *O, The Oprah Magazine* Brand Ambassador and is a board member of the Black Travel Alliance. In addition, she is an Amazon bestselling author for her series of travel e-books and a public speaker.

PROVING ALL THE NAYSAYERS WRONG
KARI DEPHILLIPS

"I'm a real sleeper and people underestimate me a lot, but I'm kind of okay with that."

Kari DePhillips is an entrepreneur and CEO of The Content Factory, a thriving content creation and search engine optimization (SEO) company. She has eschewed the typical brick-and-mortar business concept and instead runs her company remotely, which allows her to travel the world and work from anywhere.

Long before she found success in entrepreneurship, however, she was a young girl growing up on an orchard in a rural farm town in California. Pigs and chickens ran around the property freely, but she and her mother were stuck in a chaotic and abusive household.

"My mom was always a great source of inspiration to me," Kari said. "She died when I was 22 years old. The tragedy for me in her death was the life unlived. She had so much potential. She was funny and brilliant and so kind. She could've done anything. The day she died, my dad got the divorce papers in the mail. She never got to break free."

But Kari did. The second she could legally leave home, she did, waving goodbye to her hometown just after high school. She moved across the country to Pennsylvania, to attend a women's college and start her career. But when her mother got sick, she left school to care for her until her death, and never found the money to finish her degree. Instead, she found herself working a job in advertising she thought was her dream job—until her manager sexually harassed her.

"He put his hand on my thigh and rubbed it during a client pitch meeting," she said. "I reported it to my male superior, who ran it up to the two male owners of the company, who made him apologize to me. But he remained my manager after that."

Kari knew she had to quit. She was over the double standards which so often applied to women in office environments and the pressure she felt to spend time every morning doing her hair and makeup. She was sick of being judged by her appearance instead of her work performance, done with having to deal with sleazy bosses to keep a paycheck, and no longer interested in giving someone else the power to determine her level of income.

So, she started thinking about what else might be out there for her. At the time she was dating a man who worked as a freelance writer, and she loved his lifestyle. He was always flying around the world, staying in nice hotels, and being paid for it.

"I was asking him, 'How did you get into this?'" she said. "I think I could be a freelance writer. And he said, 'I'm not gonna tell you. Everyone thinks they can be a writer, and they can't. You can figure it out on your own.'"

So, she did. The two broke up and Kari began looking for content writing jobs on Craigslist, scouring the site for opportunities, sometimes sending up to 50 pitches a day.

"Immediately I started getting hired even though I had no experience," Kari said. "Within three contracts, the jobs came easier and I started getting regular clients. In three months, I replaced my advertising income and quit that job."

Many of the gigs she acquired in those early days required writing for search engine optimization. As she went further into a career in editorial, she started noticing the lack of women working in SEO and recognized it as an opportunity.

In 2010, she formally launched The Content Factory. It took off, growing quickly as one of the only woman-owned businesses in the space. Today it is one of the largest companies of its kind.

"I started with five hundred dollars that I put toward a website,"

Kari said. "Last year I was named one of the top three women in the industry. Today the Content Factory website generates over one million dollars in revenue a year, and we're able to replicate that level of success for our clients."

Her accomplishments as a CEO have disrupted a male-dominated industry and employed a team of talented content creators around the world.

From the company's inception, Kari adopted the remote workplace model for all her employees and embraced travel. In 2017, with the help of a friend, Kari launched a podcast called *Workationing*, that helps others escape the 9-5 grind and become digital nomads themselves.

Through everything, Kari credits her success to hard work and passion—and proving her haters wrong along the way. With no college education, no experience in entrepreneurship, and sometimes no clue as to whether she was doing things the "right" way, those naysayers were often plentiful. But Kari never listened.

"My dad always told me I wasn't going to amount to much, college professors sometimes said it, certainly ex-boyfriends at times, who are exes for a reason," she said. "I'm a real sleeper and people tend to underestimate me a lot, but I'm kind of okay with that. I do my best work from a place of 'fuck you.'"

BIO: Kari DePhillips is the CEO of The Content Factory, a digital marketing agency that specializes in PR and SEO. She's also the co-host of the *Workationing* podcast, which follows her adventures working around the world with friends while knocking items off their bucket lists. Kari's been named a "limit-breaking female founder" by Thrive Global, a "CEO who takes job perks to the max" by NBC News and a "digital nomad role model" by *Glamour* magazine. In her spare time, she mentors other femmes in SEO via the Sisters in SEO Facebook group she cofounded, which at over 8k members has become the largest network of women in the industry.

....

TOOLS TO TRIUMPH

The Prevailers featured in this chapter were all chosen for their ability to resurrect their lives in the face of abuse, tragedy, and loss. While each person's journey in processing and working through trauma are personal, there are some similarities in how these power women made it through. Here are some clear and specific strategies they used.

1. **They saw themselves through the eyes of their loved ones**

   Amanda Matthews may never have left her abusive marriage if it hadn't been for her children. But seeing life through their eyes and understanding that, if she stayed, they'd have to live through what she had had to live through, made all the difference.

   Can you look at yourself through the lens of the people who love you? Can you give yourself the same grace you'd give a loved one?

2. **They established what they didn't want for themselves**

   Stephanie Plymale didn't know what her future would look like as a child living in the backseat of her mother's car. But she knew what she *didn't* want. Using this as a baseline helped her move closer to things that brought her joy, happiness, and stability (her marriage, her business, her work in interior design).

   You may also find yourself unable to control much of the circumstances of your environment. You may still be growing up in your childhood home, for example, unable to move out yet but desperate to do so. You might be stuck in a marriage you cannot leave because you are not financially independent. Still, I implore you to spend a few minutes writing out what you *don't* want in your life. What would you let go of, if you were starting over? What causes you pain, confusion, hurt right now? What would you remove if you could rewrite your life?

3. **They went on journeys to get to know themselves**

When Rae Master left her religion, she found herself free to explore anything that interested her. Since she didn't really know what she did or didn't like, she let herself experiment: if an idea popped into her head, she'd try it. Through this process, for example, she realized that she loved reading, but she hated pottery.

Challenge yourself to try little things, even if that means just exploring your options. Watch a few videos on YouTube. Take a writing class from your local community college. Give yourself the permission and the space to play. What have you always wanted to do but never have?

4. **They built a support system**

When other students were telling Nadeen White that she only got into college because of affirmative action, she turned to her supportive family who encouraged her to ignore the haters, keep her head down and put in the work. When she was breaking out in hives from the stress of school, she turned to a group of students who understood that pressure.

All of us need support, and these days there are plenty of ways to find it. If you do not have a support network, create support by interacting with a community online. Invest in a therapist or mental health team, or a life or business coach. It is imperative you create this baseline for yourself. Where do you turn to for support? How can you expand that network?

5. **They put themselves out there**

Kari DePhillips had no experience as a freelance writer when she decided she wanted to be one. That didn't stop her from throwing everything at her dream—applying to nearly every opportunity she could find online, up to 50 per day. Too often the fear of failure keeps us from even trying. Instead, go *Towanda* at it and fire in rapid succession. Don't just apply for one job, apply for dozens. Put yourself out there!

LESSONS LEARNED

I spent nearly 1,500 hours interviewing women from around the world for this project and our podcast, also called *Tell Her She Can't*. What I have found without question is this:

1. ***Your story is important, and it matters.***

   Many of the women interviewed for this book said something along the lines of, "Oh, well, compared to *her*, my story is nothing." Every life lived, every experience, every pain, every emotion, is valid. Your story is important, and it matters. No matter how "good" or "bad" you think you've had it, you are your own strong, special person on your own journey. Don't compare yourself to anyone else. Everything you have done and lived through has brought you to this moment of change, realization and empowerment.

2. ***You absolutely can.***

   Life is messy, unpredictable, and impermanent. Don't deprive the world of your dreams for one second longer. Start the business. Buy the plane ticket. Make the phone call you've been putting off for years. Invest in what it takes to heal, learn and move forward. Prioritize yourself and your happiness. You absolutely can, and you absolutely will.

3. ***You have to treat yourself with love.***

   You can't change your past, your birth family, or the environment you were raised in. You can't change the ways you might've been failed or betrayed. But you can shift your

TELL HER SHE CAN'T

perspective. You can treat *yourself* with kindness. You don't have to forgive anyone that you're not ready to, but you absolutely should forgive yourself.

Everyone always says to "love ourselves," but no one actually tells us *how*. For me, it wasn't so instinctual. Like healing, self-love is a gradual process. One night, I actually found myself Googling, "How to really love yourself."

The predictable answers came back: create positive affirmations, eat healthy food, exercise, sleep better, practice gratitude. I've done all of these things, and while they're all awesome, what's really made a difference for me is something different altogether: *surrendering*.

The Gold We Hold Within

Okay, mountain, I think. *Now it's just you and me.*

Once again, I am climbing up a mountain that I have no business being on. Today it's Adam's Peak in Sri Lanka, a grueling vertical climb composed of over 5,500 uneven, steep, rocky steps.

"Just make it to that light post," I say softly to myself. "Just make it to that next tree." I gain a little momentum before I have to double over, gasping for air. This cycle repeats every 10 or so steps. I am screaming internally so loudly I fear the sound might actually escape my lips and become real.

I am the world's most reluctant hiker, a woman who routinely finds herself doing things at the behest of her friends, simply because she doesn't want to be left out. I feel like a giant fool. I had all but decided not to do this hike. But when Katie, Kat, and Sarah woke me up at 2:30 a.m. to begin packing for the hike in the darkness, I knew I couldn't stay in bed. Hanging back would only be confirmation that I am not enough for this task: not thin enough, not fit enough, not strong enough. I am here to prove myself wrong, and what better a setting, than this, a holy pilgrimage.

At the top of *this* mountain, they say, is a giant footprint. Buddhists believe it is the footprint of Lord Buddha. Christians and Muslims believe it is the footprint of Adam, created the moment he first stepped on Earth after being cast from the Garden of Eden. Hindus believe it is the footprint of Shiva. Over 20k pilgrims come here annually from around the world to see it and have for at least 200 years. This is Sri Lanka's most holy mountain, *Sri Pada*. No other mountain in the world is as religiously significant to as many different groups of people. It is truly a marvel of this planet.

We set out at 3 a.m., and in the darkness, the excitement is palpable. Other hikers join us on our ascent, which begins slowly at first. The steps are spread out so that you take three flat paces before a climb. The moon and Katie's headlamp illuminate our path. Our goal is to make it to the top before sunrise at 6 a.m., which gives us three full hours to climb, but the terrain gets steeper by the minute. Completing this pilgrimage signifies a dedication to one's faith and the pursuit of love and knowledge. I know I am right where I need to be.

An hour in, things start to get rough. Katie helps me when I struggle with side cramps by turning everything into a game. "How many steps until that light post?" she asks. I pant out a guess. "Let's see how fast we can get to that telephone pole!" she says. I am a wheezy mess, stopping to use my inhaler and catch my breath so often that eventually I just tell her to join the others and go on without me. Wanting to catch the sunrise, she does.

I am alone now in this fight, with only my thoughts and breath to keep me company. Only I can get myself up the next 3k or so stairs. On the path along with me are several local elderly women, who are making this trek in flip-flops and long skirts.

I can tell that some have been on this mountain for several days. They remind me that there's no right or wrong way to do this hike, or any other. Up, up, up we all go.

If they can do it, I can do it, I think. Yet with each set of steps comes another, and I am assaulted by thoughts that say otherwise.

> *You can't do this; you don't have it in you.*
> *You have no business even being here.*

You're not even religious!

I take slow and deliberate breaths, but these words continue washing over me, wearing me down. Two hours into the hike and I am emotionally and physically spent.

There is something transcendental that happens after hours of being pushed past your physical breaking point in a situation like this. Your vision gets a little blurry, your brain a little wobbly from so many steps at altitude. Your breathing becomes rhythmic. It is a meditative, angry calm: the perfect setting for an internal showdown.

> *Whose words am I hearing anyway? Am I really here again, not loving myself? Do I really believe I'm not capable or worthy, and that I can't do this? Or did I inherit these thoughts after so many years of trying (and failing) to prove my worth to my step family? So many years of hoping (and failing) that my father would choose me over drinking? So many years of feeling like I wasn't anyone's priority?*

> *Climb. Climb. Cry.*
> *Climb. Climb. Cry.*

Three hours in, and I have accepted my own defeat. The bad thoughts have won. I am sitting on the stairs now, fully sobbing into my hands. I can't do it. I'm not enough. I'm not strong enough. I never was, I never will be.

"Hey bud," I hear Kat say. She's appeared out of nowhere, having doubled back to check on me. She must've climbed down a quarter of the mountain just to find me. I turn to her and ugly cry. "I don't know if I can do this," I sob, snot flowing into my light pink scarf.

"I think you can," she says. "But it's up to you." I stand up, slowly, encouraged by this thought.

Safe. Worthy. Infinite.

These words become my mantra again as I push forward. I am focused on nothing else but the next step. Not my blood, pulsing at the tip of my nose. Not my feet, crying from uneven cobblestones. Not my thighs, locked into place after hours of climbing. I climb with fervor, desperate to prove to myself that I can do it, that I am capable and lovable and *enough*.

As we get closer to the top, however, my next crushing defeat comes. The sky is getting lighter. The sun has started peeking out from the horizon—I didn't make it to the top by sunrise. I start to feel myself slipping back, back into the bad place. I'm such a loser that I am the only one of my friends to not make it to the top in time.

I throw my body across the top of the metal handrail and audibly cry, a squealing sort of pinched pain, a sound that I have never heard myself make before. This is the end of the road. I fought, I climbed, and I was not enough.

Cloaked in shame, I look up and realize people around me suddenly seem to *see* me. I feel a twinge of embarrassment at my outburst and my position, bent over a metal railway. Climbers ahead of me are looking back, some with pity, others with understanding, knowing that I'm in the midst of battling demons that they can't help with.

But one person doesn't turn away: a young monk, clad in flowing orange robes. He's standing motionless above me, saying nothing. Waiting.

Suddenly, I don't feel like crying anymore. Instead, it all goes still. The thoughts abate. My legs stop hurting. My heart rate calms and my shoulders release. I *surrender*.

I completely give in to this moment and to this mountain. I close my eyes for a moment and cede to my physical body; to all of its beauty and its flaws, to all of its strength and limitations.

The monk stretches out his hand to me, and with his help, I pull myself from the metal railing and stand up straight. He nods once, slowly, then turns around and starts to walk up the mountain again. Obediently, I follow him in silence. He looks over his shoulder periodically to see if I'm still with him.

After surrender, comes laughter. The fact that a monk is pulling me up the most holy of mountains is not lost on me. I actually *am* enough. I actually *can* do this. It feels absurd to have ever thought otherwise! Step by step, I follow him. Up, up, up. Twenty stairs later and I realize, we're done. We were at the top all along.

Elation spills from my eyes as I stand in line to ring the gong at the mountain's peak. Kat and I find our friends and join them just in time to absorb one of the most stunning sunrises I have ever seen.

Years later I would learn that Adam's Peak is famous for optical sunrise illusions. Light rays from the sun get reflected like a mirror as they reach and surpass the dense cloud cover at the top of the mountain, creating the effect of showing hikers multiple sunrises. It's a phenomenon known as "total internal reflection." I was just in time to experience it.

Sometimes you have to prove to yourself over and over that you can. Here above the soft pink cloud cover, the morning sun spills over us and turns everything to gold. Gold on my safe, tear-stained face. Gold on my tired, worthy legs. Gold, on my hand, held over my infinite heart, in thanks. Gold, across everything I thought I wasn't and the expanse of everything I am and will be.

Gold.
Shimmering.
Defiant.
Free.

RESOURCES

The following are links to supporting articles about the women featured, and/or their personal stories. They are organized by chapter and by person, in order of appearance.

You Have to Love Yourself

Bhutan's Gross National Happiness Index
https://ophi.org.uk/policy/gross-national-happiness-index/

Honoring Guru Rinpoche and His Lasting Legacy in Bhutan on His Birthday
https://www.dailybhutan.com/article/honouring-guru-rinpoche-and-his-lasting-legacy-in-bhutan-on-his-birthday

Fire Destroys Famed Monastery in the Himalayas
https://www.nytimes.com/1998/04/22/world/fire-destroys-famed-monastery-in-the-himalayas.html

The Resilient Journey

Jaisalmer "Golden City"
https://en.wikipedia.org/wiki/Jaisalmer

Challenging Systems to Create Impactful Change
THE CHANGEMAKERS

The White House Hosts a Travel Blogger Summit on Study Abroad and Global Citizenship
https://obamawhitehouse.archives.gov/blog/2014/12/15/white-house-hosts-travel-blogger-summit-study-abroad-and-global-citizenship

SHANNON ALLEN

Grown
https://www.grown.org/

JANICE LINTZ

New York City Taxi and Limousine Commission: Hearing Loops
https://www1.nyc.gov/assets/tlc/downloads/pdf/proposed_rules_anti_assault_and_hearing_loop_decal.pdf

Hearing Access and Innovations
https://www.hearingaccess.com/

New York Taxi, Limousine Commission Hearing Loop Pilot Project Underway
https://www.hearingreview.com/hearing-products/implants-bone-conduction/cochlear-implants/new-york-taxi-limousine-commission-hearing-loop-pilot-project-underway

MTA Induction Loops at Station Booths
http://web.mta.info/accessibility/station_booths.htm

All in! Accessibility in the National Park Service
https://www.nps.gov/aboutus/upload/All_In_Accessibility_in_the_NPS_2015-2020_FINAL.pdf
https://www.nps.gov/features/hfc/guidelines/#h.1gxnft3n0qec

Delta Air Lines
https://janceslintz.files.wordpress.com/2015/04/deltasky-515.pdf

Build-a-Bear
https://www.hearingaccess.com/?page_id=324

https://www.buildabear.com/plush-hearing-aid/009728.html

TAYLOR LINLOFF

The Nature of Things
https://www.cbc.ca/natureofthings/

Data and Statistics on Autism Spectrum Disorder
https://www.cdc.gov/ncbddd/autism/data.html

Females with Autism are Underdiagnosed, Underrepresented in Research
https://www.wpr.org/females-autism-are-underdiagnosed-under-represented-research

Brain Changes Suggest Autism Starts in the Womb
https://www.npr.org/sections/health-shots/2014/03/26/294446735/brain-changes-suggest-autism-starts-in-the-womb

Local Autism Advocate appears on CBS Special
https://www.invernessoran.ca/entertainment/1480-local-autism-advocate

Autistics Aloud
http://autismnovascotia.ca/autistics-aloud

National Autism Strategy
https://www.canada.ca/en/public-health/services/diseases/autism-spectrum-disorder-asd/national-strategy.html

GAELYNN LEA

Meet Gaelynn Lea, the 2016 NPR's Tiny Desk Contest Winner
https://www.npr.org/2016/03/03/469034857/meet-gaelynn-lea-the-2016-tiny-desk-contest-winner

What is the American's With Disability Act?
https://adata.org/learn-about-ada

Osteogenesis Imperfecta
https://www.hopkinsmedicine.org/health/conditions-and-diseases/osteogenesis-imperfecta

Gaelynn Lea's Website
https://violinscratches.com/

Finding Purpose: Turning Adversity into Advocacy
THE CHAMPIONS

ADRIANA MALLOZZI

Puffin Innovations
https://puffininno.com/

Hacking for Those with Disabilities
https://news.mit.edu/2015/perspective-athack-assistive-technologies-hackathon-0601

FROSWA' BOOKER-DREW

Proximity + Presence: Social Capital and Polarization (Tedx)
https://www.ted.com/talks/froswa_booker_drew_proximity_presence_social_capital_and_polarization

World Vision
https://www.worldvision.org/

State Fair of Texas
https://bigtex.com/

Froswa' Booker-Drew: A Champion for South Dallas Nonprofits
https://www.dallasdoinggood.com/doing-good/froswa-booker-drew-a-champion-for-south-dallas-nonprofits

LESLIE PITT

Project LOLO
https://www.projectlolo.org/

Lolo's Superpower
https://www.amazon.com/Lolos-Superpower-Leslie-Pitt/
dp/1634891635

WILLOW HILL

Belonging is at our core
https://www.airbnb.com/diversity/belonging

Scout Lab
https://www.scoutlab.com/

CONSTANZA ROEDER

Hearts Need Art
https://heartsneedart.org/

Cultivating Inner Fire and Discovering Your Strength
THE WARRIORS

Trichotillomania
https://www.nhs.uk/conditions/trichotillomania/

PAMM MCFADDEN

http://www.onlyacarryon.com

EMMA SOTHERN

What you need to know about Alopecia Areata
https://www.naaf.org/alopecia-areata

Lady Alopecia
https://www.ladyalopecia.com/

ANGELA BRADFORD

**Angela Bradford of World Financial Group on Why a Person
in Leadership Needs to Develop Mental Toughness**
https://medium.com/authority-magazine/angela-bradford-of-

world-financial-group-why-a-person-in-leadership-needs-to-de-
velop-mental-6c038a36e9cf

OLGA MARIA CZARKOWSKI

Latinas Who Travel
https://latinaswhotravel.com/our-founder-latina-world-traveler-
olga-maria-dreams-in-heels/

Heidi Siefkas
When All Balls Drop: The Upside to Losing Everything
https://www.amazon.com/dp/B00MGYVG42/

Heidi's Website
http://www.heidisiefkas.com

Rewriting the Rules - Becoming Unstoppable
THE TRAILBLAZERS

Tips for Women Traveling Solo: Q&A with Kelly Lewis
https://www.nytimes.com/2016/08/28/travel/tips-kelly-lewis-go-
girl-guides.html?_r=2

Meet the Women Changing Travel
https://adventure.com/women-changing-travel/

Kelly Lewis (and her story)
http://www.gokellylewis.com

SANDRA HART

Life Over Sixty with Sandra
https://www.youtube.com/channel/UCsyeT-
5Jf3-Ak51Udv1XIjLg

Romper Room and Sandra
https://sandrashart.com/2017/01/07/unexpected-mo-
ments-in-time/

In Schizophrenia's Wake, a Son Laments the Father Who Might've Been

https://www.bbrfoundation.org/content/schizophrenias-wake-son-laments-father-who-might-have-been

Behind the Magic Mirror: The Searing Memoir of a Romper Room Teacher

https://www.amazon.com/Behind-Magic-Mirror-Searing-Teacher/dp/0971552509/

MIRNA VALERIO

Mirna's Story

https://themirnavator.com/

Ultra: Mirna Valerio

https://www.runnersworld.com/runners-stories/a21070665/ultra/

Meet 2018 National Geographic Traveler of the Year

https://www.nationalgeographic.com/adventure/features/adventurers-of-the-year/2018/mirna-valerio-ultramarathon-runner/

A Beautiful Work in Progress

https://www.amazon.com/dp/B01N21CG4I/

LUCIANA FAULHABER

Luciana's website and work

http://www.lucianafaulhaber.com/

Stars Making a Social Impact: Why Luciana Faulhaber is making films that raise awareness about the plight of the vulnerable among us

https://medium.com/authority-magazine/stars-making-a-social-impact-why-luciana-faulhaber-is-making-films-that-raise-awareness-about-the-33faf1560bcc

Luciana Faulhaber IMDB

https://www.imdb.com/name/nm3445312/

JARRY LEE

Meet Jarry Lee
http://voyagela.com/interview/meet-jarry-lee-jarry-lee-santa-monica/

Jarry Lee's Website
https://www.jarrylee.com/

Jarry Lee on Instagram
https://www.jarrylee.com/

KITTIE WESTON-KNAUER

Why don't you try it? How the oldest female BMX racer broke into the sport
https://www.npr.org/2018/05/11/609738535/why-don-t-you-try-it-how-the-oldest-u-s-female-bmx-racer-broke-into-the-sport

Kittie Weston-Knauer, the Grio100
https://www.iowapublicradio.org/show/talk-of-iowa/2011-02-09/kittie-weston-knauer-thegrio-100

Meet the Oldest Female BMX Racer in the World
https://www.cnn.com/videos/health/2017/10/18/fit-nation-bmx-grandma-kittie-weston-knauer.cnn

Children & Family Urban Movement
https://cfum.org/

Running Faster Toward Your Fear
THE ADVENTURERS

AJ Hackett Macau Tower Bungee Jump
https://www.ajhackett.com/macau/

FELICITY ASTON

Britain Felicity Aston Becomes First Person to Manually Ski Solo Across Antarctica
https://www.theguardian.com/world/2012/jan/23/felicity-as-

ton-ski-solo-antarctica

First Woman to Ski Solo Across Antarctica Sets Record
https://www.worldrecordacademy.com/travel/first_woman_
to_ski_solo_across_Antarctica_Felicity_Aston_sets_world_re-
cord_112692.html

Arctic Foxes Greenland Quest
http://www.felicityaston.co.uk/arctic-foxes-greenland-quest
First woman to cross Antarctica: I've never felt so alone
https://www.cnn.com/travel/article/felicity-aston-antarctic-ex-
plorer/index.html

CAZZY MAGENNIS

Cazzy's Travel Blog
https://www.dreambigtravelfarblog.com/authors/cazzy-magennis

ASHLEY BARTNER

Wildest Dreams with Oprah
http://www.oprah.com/own-where-are-they-now/15-biggest-
wildest-dreams-come-true/all

Looking for authentic Italy? Try Le Marche
https://www.forbes.com/sites/liviahengel/2019/11/12/look-
ing-for-authentic-italy-try-le-marche/?sh=19be66df1b0e

La Tavola Marche
https://www.latavolamarche.com/

JESSICA NABONGO

**Get to know Jessica Nabongo, the First Documented Black
Woman to Travel to Every Country in the World**
https://www.travelandleisure.com/trip-ideas/solo-travel/jessica-
nabongo-catch-me-if-you-can

The Catch Me If You Can
https://thecatchmeifyoucan.com/

LAUREN PEARS

The Planet Edit
https://www.theplanetedit.com/

Building Resolve to Never Doubt Your Vision
THE VISIONARIES

MICKELA MALLOZZI

Bare Feet with Mickela Mallozzi
https://www.travelbarefeet.com/

Mickela's Story
https://www.travelbarefeet.com/my-story

AMY GIGI ALEXANDER

Panorama: The Journal of Intelligent Travel
http://www.panoramajournal.org/

Why I Travel: My #YesAllWomen
http://www.worldhum.com/features/travel-stories/why-i-travel-yesallwomen-20140605/

NATALIA 'SAW LADY' PARUZ

'Saw Lady' Website
https://sawlady.com/

Videos of 'Saw Lady' Playing
https://www.youtube.com/channel/UCMEH-Cv9D1T-jPp6As1vE7Zg

What is the Musical Saw?
https://sawlady.com/what-is-the-musical-saw/

About Musical Saws
https://en.wikipedia.org/wiki/Musical_saw

Largest Musical Saw Ensemble - Guinness Book of

World Records

https://www.guinnessworldrecords.com/world-records/largest-musical-saw-ensemble

New York City Musical Saw Festival

http://musicalsawfestival.org/

ALEXA FISCHER

Alexa Fischer IMDB

https://www.imdb.com/name/nm1268419/

Inspirational Women in Hollywood: How Actress Alexa Fischer Aims to Help People Build Their Confidence

https://medium.com/authority-magazine/inspirational-women-in-hollywood-how-actress-alexa-fischer-aims-to-help-people-build-their-9a43bc010c5

Wishbeads

https://www.wishbeads.com/

Wishbeads Kickstarter

https://www.kickstarter.com/projects/wishbeads/wishbeads-write-wear-watch-your-wishes-come-true

SANDY STEIN

Finder's Key Purse

https://finderskeypurse.com/

Sandy Stein: The Flight Attendant Who Soared Higher Than Any Flight

https://medium.com/@ScottAmyx/sandy-stein-the-flight-attendant-who-soared-higher-than-any-flight-cc317feac917

An Unexpected Descent into Entrepreneurship

https://www.creditcards.com/credit-card-news/small-business-profile-finders-key-purse/

Surviving Literally Anything
THE PREVAILERS

AMANDA MATTHEWS

Amanda's ebook
https://www.amazon.com/Shattered-Sanctuary-Amanda-Matthews-ebook/dp/B07SNGQXNC

STEPHANIE PLYMALE

American Daughter: A Memoir
https://www.amazon.com/American-Daughter-Stephanie-Thornton-Plymale/dp/0063054337/

'American Daughter' Author Shares Shocking Secrets of Her Childhood
https://www.today.com/video/-american-daughter-author-shares-shocking-secrets-of-her-childhood-78548037596

RAE MASTER

Jehovah's Witness Beliefs
https://www.britannica.com/topic/Jehovahs-Witnesses/Beliefs

When Religions Leads to Trauma
https://www.nytimes.com/2019/02/05/well/mind/religion-trauma-lgbt-gay-depression-anxiety.html

Rae Master's Website
https://raemaster.com/

NADEEN WHITE

National Honor Society
https://www.nhs.us/

The Sophisticated Life
https://thesophisticatedlife.com/

Nadeen on CNN

https://www.youtube.com/watch?v=SV0cBQdoEJM

O Magazine Brand Ambassadors
https://omaginsider.com/o-mag-insiders/meet-the-insiders/

KARI DEPHILLIPS

The Content Factory
https://www.contentfac.com/

Workationing
https://workationing.com/

The Gold We Hold Within

Why You Should Climb 5,500 Steps in the Dark
https://www.fodors.com/world/asia/sri-lanka/experiences/news/
why-you-should-climb-5500-steps-in-the-dark

Adam's Peak
https://wikitravel.org/en/Adam%27s_Peak
Total Internal Reflection
https://www.britannica.com/science/total-internal-reflection

Additional Reading

Want to delve a bit deeper into some of the topics we covered? The following books have either been mentioned in this book, or are just awesome.

The Power by Naomi Alderman

Daring Greatly: How the Courage to Be Vulnerable Transforms the Way We Live, Love, Parent, and Lead by Brene Brown

Everything is Figureoutable by Marie Forleo

Big Magic by Elizabeth Gilbert

The Rabbit Effect: Live Longer, Healthier and Happier with the Groundbreaking Science of Kindness by Kelli Harding

The Confidence Gap: A Guide to Overcoming Fear and Self-

Doubt by Russ Harris

Feel the Fear and Do it Anyway by Susan Jeffries

Finding Meaning: The Sixth Stage of Grief by David Kesler

The Crossroads of Should and Must by Elle Luna

The Power of Your Subconscious Mind by Joseph Murphy

Breath by James Nestor

You are a Badass by Jen Sincero

Do It Scared: Finding the Courage to Face Your Fears, Overcome Adversity and Create a Life You Love by Ruth Soukup

ACKNOWLEDGMENTS

First and foremost, thank you to the brave, resilient, badass ladies who volunteered their stories for this book. You have inspired me, encouraged me, moved me, and you have given my life's story a greater purpose. I am forever thankful to have met you.

Thank you to Molly Leibowitz for your lifelong friendship and support, and for making me jump off the Macau Tower. What a memory! To Adrienne Knoll, Amanda Bova, and Jessica Swanson, thank you for holding it TF down and reading this book again and again as I shaped and molded it. Stephanie, Kelsey, Jewel, Mallory, Allison, Maya, Erica, Mikey, and Lauren, thank you for letting me ask your opinions on a thousand things!

Amy Gigi Alexander and Melissa Bloom, thank you for your sharp edits and encouragement. Shannon Kaiser, thank you for your mentorship and friendship. To the team at Book Launchers, you rock! Elise, thank you for being a masterful editor on our podcast.

To my mother and father: this book 100 percent could not have happened without you. I would have certainly chickened out at the thought of sharing some of these stories had it not been for your unwavering support. I love you both so much.

To my community of intrepid female travelers—thank you for helping champion this project. There's not one entrepreneur in this world who "does it" all alone. The list of my IOUs for this book is one mile long. We did it!

Last but certainly not least, to Nate, my big, sweet love: I'm so lucky to have you in my life. Your unwavering support and encouragement mean everything to me. Thank you for being a progressive, kind, badass feminist of a man, and for bringing so much joy into my world. I love you.

To every little girl currently living in an environment that tells you that you can't: one day you will. You've got this.